Plant-Based Slow Cooker Cookbook for Beginners

The Ultimate Guide with 1800 Days of Easy,
Tasty & Wholesome Recipes to Support a Healthy
Lifestyle on a Vegetarian Diet. Includes a 28-Day Meal Plan

Amanda Ray

© Copyright 2025 - All rights reserved.

The content contained within this book may not be reproduced, duplicated, or transmitted without direct written permission from the author or publisher.

Under no circumstances will any blame or legal responsibility be held against the publisher or author for any damages, reparations, or monetary losses due to the information contained within this book, either directly or indirectly.

Legal Notice:

This book is copyright-protected. It is only for personal use. You cannot amend, distribute, sell, use, quote, or paraphrase any part or the content within it without the consent of the author or publisher.

Disclaimer Notice:

Please note that the information contained within this document is for educational and entertainment purposes only. All efforts have been made to present accurate, up-to-date, reliable, and complete information. No warranties of any kind are declared or implied. Readers acknowledge that the author is not engaged in the rendering of legal, financial, medical, or professional advice. The content within this book has been derived from various sources. Please consult a licensed professional before attempting any techniques outlined in this book.

By reading this document, the reader agrees that under no circumstances is the author responsible for any losses, direct or indirect, that are incurred as a result of the use of the information contained within this document, including, but not limited to, errors, omissions, or inaccuracies.

Table of Content

Introduction 6

Chapter 1: Introduction to Plant-Based Slow Cooking 7
The Power of Plants: A Whole-Food Approach 7
Why the Slow Cooker Is Your Best Ally 7
Rethinking Convenience: Healthy Meals Without the Hassle 7
Unlocking Nutrition Through Low-Heat Cooking 8
Building a Mindful Kitchen Routine 8

Chapter 2: Morning Warmth 10
Creamy Coconut Quinoa Porridge 10
Maple Chia Oatmeal Delight 11
Cinnamon Apple Buckwheat Bowl 11
Almond Banana Millet Mash 12
Spiced Pumpkin Amaranth Porridge .. 12
Golden Turmeric Oats 13
Blueberry Lemon Breakfast Quinoa 13
Peanut Butter Cacao Oats 14
Coconut Date Breakfast Rice 14
Warm Fig & Hazelnut Farro 15
Vanilla Pear Millet Bowl 15
Strawberry Basil Chia Pudding 16
Banana Bread Breakfast Oats 16
Apple Pie Cauliflower Bowl 17
Tropical Mango Quinoa Mash 17
Lavender Vanilla Barley Bowl 18
Sweet Potato Pie Oats 18

Chapter 3: Small Bites 19
Smoky Maple Chickpeas 19
Slow-Roasted Spiced Nuts 20
Buffalo Cauliflower Bites 20
Stuffed Bell Pepper Scoops 21
Ginger-Garlic Edamame 21
Slow-Cooked Salsa Dip 22
Herb & Olive Bean Medley 22
Sweet Potato Tot Cups 23
Sticky Sesame Mushrooms 23
Zesty Lentil Poppers 24
Jalapeño Corn Dip 24
Vegan Spinach Artichoke Dip 25
Cashew Carrot Spread 25
Roasted Red Pepper Hummus 26
Coconut Curry Popcorn Mix 26
BBQ Pulled Mushroom Sliders 27
Caramelized Onion Bruschetta 27

Chapter 4: Cozy Bowls 28
Rustic Tomato Lentil Soup 28
Sweet Potato Corn Chowder 29
Thai-Inspired Coconut Soup 29
Spicy Brown Rice & Mushroom Stew 30
Creamy Broccoli & Pea Soup 30
Moroccan Chickpea Stew 31
Butternut Squash Apple Soup 31
Lemon Dill Split Pea Soup 32
Italian White Bean Stew 32
Zucchini Basil Bisque 33
Curried Carrot Ginger Soup 33
Roasted Red Pepper Soup 34
Kale & Potato Comfort Stew 34
Cabbage and Fennel Soup 35
Black Garlic Veggie Broth 35

Chapter 5: Hearty Plates 36
Rustic Tofu Pot Roast 36

Lentil & Root Veg Shepherd's Pie......... 37
Stuffed Squash with Wild Rice 37
Tofu and Veggie Stroganoff 38
Mediterranean Chickpea Bake.............. 38
Mushroom Bourguignon........................ 39
Slow-Cooked Eggplant Parmesan.......... 39
Creamy Polenta with Ratatouille 40
Sweet Potato and Peanut Casserole..... 40
Balsamic Glazed Cauliflower Steaks 41
Tamari Tempeh & Veggie Skillet 41
Portobello and Barley Bake 42
Vegan Jambalaya.................................... 42
Cheesy Vegan Cauliflower Gratin......... 43
Slow Cooker Stuffed Cabbage Rolls..... 43

Chapter 6: Flavorful Sides............44
Lemon Herb Quinoa Pilaf....................... 44
Garlic Roasted Cauliflower Rice............ 45
Sweet & Spicy Glazed Carrots............... 45
Creamy Mashed Parsnips...................... 46
Savory Green Bean Almondine.............. 46
Apple Cider Brussels Sprouts 47
Spiced Basmati Rice Medley 47
Ginger Sesame Bok Choy....................... 48
Herbed Sweet Potato Mash................... 48
Caramelized Onion and Kale 49
Maple Glazed Acorn Squash................... 49
Wild Mushroom Rice Blend 50
Rosemary Garlic Fingerlings 50

Chapter 7: Bold & Saucy..................51
Chickpea Tikka Masala 51
Thai Red Lentil Curry 52
Spicy Black Bean Chili............................ 52
Coconut Sweet Potato Curry................ 53
Jamaican Jerk Veggie Stew 53
Butternut Chickpea Curry..................... 54
White Bean & Kale Chili........................ 54
Ethiopian Berbere Lentils 55
Creamy Cashew Cauliflower Curry 55
Smoky Tempeh Chili 56
Green Thai Vegetable Curry 56

Chapter 8: Plant-Powered Grains. 57
Cajun Black-Eyed Peas 57
Ginger Turmeric Lentils......................... 58
Cuban Mojo Black Beans....................... 58
Brown Rice & Pinto Bowl..................... 59
Lemony Farro and Fava Beans............... 59

Smoky Cannellini with Spinach............ 60
Savory Chickpeas with Wild Rice......... 60
Barley and Vegetable Pilaf 61
Cajun Red Beans and Rice..................... 61
Mexican-Spiced Lentil Medley...............62
Sun-Dried Tomato Quinoa 62

Chapter 9: Tangle-Free Twists 63
Creamy Vegan Mac & Peas 63
Garlic Alfredo Zucchini Pasta 64
Spaghetti Squash Primavera.................. 64
Slow-Cooked Lasagna Roll-Ups 65
Thai Peanut Noodle Bowl......................65
Mushroom Stroganoff Pasta.................. 66
Butternut Squash Shells 66
Lemon Garlic Orzo 67
Teriyaki Udon Stir-Fry 67
Creamy Tomato Penne Bake 68
Pesto Pasta with White Beans.............. 68

Chapter 10: Purely Plant-Based.....69
Braised Tofu with Root Veggies 69
Tempeh and Broccoli Stir Bowl............70
Spaghetti Squash with Lentil Sauce......70
Vegan Moroccan Tagine 71
Maple BBQ Seitan Medallions................71
Italian Vegan Stuffed Peppers................ 72
Zesty Lentil Taco Filling........................ 72
Cashew Cream Enchiladas 73
Vegan Stuffed Eggplant Boats............... 73
Miso Glazed Sweet Potatoes 74
Spiced Tofu Veggie Loaf 74
Slow Cooker Vegan "Meatballs" 75
Vegan Chickpea Bake with Avocado.... 75
Cabbage & Avocado Wrap 76
Lemon Garlic Tempeh Strips 76

Chapter 11: Sweet Comforts 77
Choco-Chia Pudding Cake..................... 77
Maple Pecan Sticky Rice 78
Spiced Apple Cobbler 78
Slow-Cooked Choco Banana Bread 79
Almond Butter Fudge Brownies 79
Coconut Vanilla Rice Pudding 80
Orange Cranberry Bread Pudding 80
Carrot Cake Oat Bars 81
Vegan Chocolate Lava Pots 81
Warm Blueberry Crumble.....................82
Cinnamon Pear Compote 82

Chapter 12: 28-Day Meal Prep Plan 83
Week 1: 83
Week 2: 83
Week 3: 84
Week 4: 84

Free Gift 85

Conclusion outline 86

References 87

Appendix 1: Measurement Conversion Chart 88

Appendix 2: Index Recipes 89
A 89
B 89
C 90
D 91
E 91
F 91
G 91
H 92
J 92
K 92
L 92
M 92
O 93
P 93
Q 93
R 93
S 94
T 94
U 94
V 94
W 94
Z 95

Notes 96

Introduction

I still remember the first time I plugged in my slow cooker intending to make an entirely plant-based meal. I wasn't a seasoned vegan, and I definitely wasn't confident in the kitchen. I just wanted to feel better—more energized, less bloated, and more in control of my health.

I had read about the benefits of a plant-based diet—lower cholesterol, better digestion, reduced inflammation—but I was intimidated. Could I really make filling, flavorful meals without meat, dairy, or eggs? Would I be stuck eating salads forever? And would my slow cooker, which had been collecting dust in the back of a cabinet, actually help me stick to this new lifestyle?

The answer surprised me.

At first, it was trial and error. I overcooked a few lentils, made a couple of stews that tasted like cardboard, and burned some rice. But I kept going. I kept experimenting. I focused on whole, simple ingredients—beans, veggies, grains, spices—and let the slow cooker do the hard work.

Then, something shifted.

Meals that once felt like a chore became something I looked forward to. My body began to respond: I had more energy, fewer cravings, and a steady sense of well-being I hadn't felt in years. Cooking became a form of self-care instead of a stressor. And plant-based eating didn't feel restrictive—it felt empowering.

That's why I created this cookbook—because I know how overwhelming it can feel when you're just starting. Maybe you're short on time, unsure where to begin, or skeptical that plant-based food can be both easy and satisfying. I promise you, it can.

This book is for beginners, just like I once was. Every recipe is slow cooker-friendly, plant-based, and designed to make your life easier, not harder. There are no fancy ingredients. No complicated steps. It's just real food that tastes good and makes you feel even better.

If you're ready to nourish your body, simplify your routine, and fall in love with the ease of slow cooking, you're in the right place.

Let's get started!

Chapter 1: Introduction to Plant-Based Slow Cooking

The Power of Plants: A Whole-Food Approach

When we talk about a whole-food, plant-based diet, we're talking about eating real food — food that comes from the earth, not a factory. That means fruits, vegetables, legumes, whole grains, nuts, and seeds. These foods are full of vitamins, minerals, fiber, and natural energy. They're simple, but they do big things for your body.

Unlike processed foods, which are often packed with added sugar, salt, and unhealthy fats, whole plant foods are rich in nutrients that support your heart, help your digestion, and keep your immune system strong. They're also naturally low in calories but high in fiber, which means you can feel full and satisfied without overeating.

Going plant-based isn't about strict rules or perfection. It's about choosing foods that make you feel good — physically, mentally, and emotionally. And the best part? There's a world of flavor waiting for you. With herbs, spices, and creative combinations, plant-based meals can be comforting, exciting, and deeply nourishing.

You don't need to be a vegan or vegetarian to benefit. Even just adding more plants to your plate can help you feel more energized, sleep better, and improve your overall health. Over time, many people notice lower blood pressure, weight loss, clearer skin, and better mood.

This cookbook is all about making those choices easy and enjoyable. By focusing on whole, plant-based ingredients, you're giving your body what it truly needs — and setting yourself up for long-term wellness.

Why the Slow Cooker Is Your Best Ally

Let's face it — cooking every day can feel like a lot. Between work, family, and everything else life throws at you, standing over a stove just isn't always realistic. That's where the slow cooker comes in — your secret weapon in the kitchen.

The slow cooker is perfect for plant-based meals. Why? Because it lets the ingredients do the work. You just throw everything in, turn it on, and walk away. Hours later, you've got a hot, hearty, home-cooked meal waiting for you — no stirring, no babysitting.

Plant-based ingredients like beans, lentils, and root vegetables cook beautifully in a slow cooker. They soak up flavor, get tender and delicious, and turn simple recipes into deeply satisfying meals. And because it uses low, steady heat, your food cooks evenly and gently, which helps preserve flavor and texture.

If you're new to cooking or new to plant-based eating, the slow cooker makes it all feel more doable. It removes the stress and gives you more freedom. You can prepare in the morning, go about your day, and come home to a meal that feels like someone else cooked it for you.

Think of your slow cooker as your cooking partner — one that's always patient, always reliable, and never burns your food. Once you get used to it, you'll wonder how you ever lived without it.

Rethinking Convenience: Healthy Meals Without the Hassle

We often think of convenience food as something that comes from a box, a drive-thru, or the freezer aisle. But true convenience — the kind that supports your health — doesn't have to come at the cost of nutrition. That's where plant-based slow cooking shines.

Imagine this: You wake up, toss a few ingredients into your slow cooker, and head out the door. By the time you're home, your kitchen smells amazing, and dinner is ready to serve. No extra pots, no scrambling at 6 p.m. to figure out what to cook. Just a warm, nourishing meal made with real food.

Plant-based slow cooking makes healthy eating easy. It's perfect for busy parents, working professionals, students — anyone who wants to eat well without spending hours in the kitchen. With a little planning, you can prepare meals in advance, freeze leftovers, and always have something wholesome ready to go.

And it's not just about saving time. Slow cooking is also budget-friendly. Dried beans, grains, and seasonal vegetables are some of the most affordable foods out there. With just a few pantry staples and a handful of fresh ingredients, you can create meals that are satisfying, filling, and good for your body.

Convenience doesn't have to mean compromise. When you use your slow cooker to make plant-based meals, you get the best of both worlds — ease and nutrition, comfort and health.

Unlocking Nutrition Through Low-Heat Cooking

You might be surprised to learn that how you cook your food affects how your body uses it. That's another reason the slow cooker is such a great tool, especially for plant-based meals.

Low, slow cooking helps preserve nutrients. When you boil or fry foods at high temperatures, some vitamins (like vitamin C and specific B vitamins) can break down. But with the gentle heat of a slow cooker, many of these nutrients stay intact. That means your meals don't just taste good — they're also packed with the nourishment your body needs.

Slow cooking also helps break down tough fibers in foods like beans, lentils, and whole grains. This makes them easier to digest and helps your body absorb the nutrients more efficiently. If you've ever felt bloated after eating legumes, the slow cooker might just be your new best friend.

Even better, slow cooking enhances natural flavors. Onions become sweeter, spices mellow and blend, and vegetables take on a melt-in-your-mouth texture. You don't need a lot of salt, oil, or sugar to make food taste amazing — just time and a little patience.

With plant-based ingredients, gentle cooking brings out the best in them. So not only are you making healthy choices, you're making them delicious too.

Building a Mindful Kitchen Routine

A big part of plant-based living is intention — being mindful of what you eat, how you cook, and how it makes you feel. Creating a routine in the kitchen that supports your goals is key to making those habits stick.

Start simple. Choose one or two days a week to prep **Ingredients:** chop vegetables, soak beans, cook a big batch of grains. Use your slow cooker for batch meals like stews, curries, or chili that you can eat throughout the week or freeze for later. Once you get into the rhythm, meal prep won't feel like a chore — it'll feel like self-care.

Another great habit? Eating with the seasons. Seasonal produce is not only fresher and tastier, but often more affordable and nutrient-rich. A slow cooker can help you make the most of seasonal veggies — from summer zucchini to winter squash.

Also, permit yourself to slow down. Not just in your cooking, but in your eating. Sit down, breathe, and enjoy the food you've made. Savor the textures and flavors. It sounds simple, but it can transform the way you relate to food.

When you cook with care and eat with intention, you connect more deeply with your body, your values, and the world around you. And that's what mindful eating is really all about.

Chapter 2: Morning Warmth

Creamy Coconut Quinoa Porridge

⏱	**Time:** 3 hours 15 minutes	🍴	**Serving Size:** 2 bowls
🍚	**Prep Time:** 10 minutes	🍲	**Cook Time:** 3 hours 5 minutes

Each Serving Has:
Calories: 290, Carbohydrates: 38g, Saturated Fat: 6g, Protein: 7g, Fat: 12g, Sodium: 70mg, Potassium: 310mg, Fiber: 5g, Sugar: 7g, Vitamin C: 2mg, Calcium: 45mg, Iron: 2.2mg

Ingredients:
- 1/2 cup [85g] uncooked quinoa, rinsed thoroughly
- 1 1/2 cups [355ml] unsweetened coconut milk
- 1/2 cup [120ml] water
- 2 tbsp maple syrup
- 1/2 tsp ground cinnamon
- 1/4 tsp ground nutmeg
- 1/4 tsp sea salt
- 1 tsp vanilla extract
- 1/4 cup [30g] chopped almonds
- 1/4 cup [30g] fresh blueberries

Directions:
1. Add the rinsed quinoa, coconut milk, and water to the slow cooker.
2. Stir in the maple syrup, cinnamon, nutmeg, and sea salt until evenly mixed.
3. Cover and cook on low for 3 hours or until the quinoa is soft and the texture is creamy.
4. After cooking, stir in the vanilla extract to add a subtle sweetness.
5. Sprinkle chopped almonds and fresh blueberries on top before serving.

Maple Chia Oatmeal Delight

Time: 3 hours 20 minutes
Serving Size: 2 bowls
Prep Time: 10 minutes
Cook Time: 3 hours 10 minutes

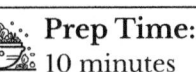

Each Serving Has:
Calories: 310, Carbohydrates: 42g, Saturated Fat: 2g, Protein: 9g, Fat: 10g, Sodium: 65mg, Potassium: 360mg, Fiber: 8g, Sugar: 9g, Vitamin C: 1mg, Calcium: 120mg, Iron: 2.6mg

Ingredients:
- 1/2 cup [40g] rolled oats
- 2 tbsp chia seeds
- 1 1/2 cups [355ml] unsweetened almond milk
- 1/2 cup [120ml] water
- 2 tbsp pure maple syrup
- 1/2 tsp ground cinnamon
- 1/4 tsp sea salt
- 1/2 tsp vanilla extract
- 1/4 cup [35g] of chopped walnuts
- 1/4 cup [30g] diced fresh apple

Directions:
1. Combine the rolled oats and chia seeds in the slow cooker.
2. Pour in the almond milk and water, then stir gently to blend.
3. Add the maple syrup, cinnamon, and sea salt to the mixture and stir to combine.
4. Cover and cook on low for 3 hours and 10 minutes until the oats are soft and the chia seeds have expanded.
5. Once cooked, stir in the vanilla extract to finish the flavor profile.
6. Top the bowls with chopped walnuts and diced fresh apple before serving.

Cinnamon Apple Buckwheat Bowl

Time: 3 hours 25 minutes
Serving Size: 2 bowls
Prep Time: 10 minutes
Cook Time: 3 hours 15 minutes

Each Serving Has:
Calories: 295, Carbohydrates: 44g, Saturated Fat: 1.5g, Protein: 8g, Fat: 7g, Sodium: 60mg, Potassium: 410mg, Fiber: 6g, Sugar: 8g, Vitamin C: 5mg, Calcium: 55mg, Iron: 2.4mg

Ingredients:
- 1/2 cup [85g] raw buckwheat groats, rinsed
- 1 1/2 cups [355ml] unsweetened oat milk
- 1/2 cup [120ml] water
- 1 medium apple, peeled and chopped
- 2 tbsp raisins
- 1 tbsp ground flaxseed
- 1 tbsp maple syrup
- 1/2 tsp ground cinnamon
- 1/4 tsp ground ginger
- 1/4 tsp sea salt
- 2 tbsp chopped pecans

Directions:
1. Add the rinsed buckwheat groats to the slow cooker along with the oat milk and water.
2. Stir in the chopped apple, raisins, ground flaxseed, maple syrup, cinnamon, ginger, and sea salt.
3. Mix well to ensure all the ingredients are combined.
4. Cover and cook on low for 3 hours and 15 minutes until the buckwheat is soft and the mixture is thickened.
5. Stir the cooked mixture to blend the softened ingredients evenly.
6. Top with chopped pecans before serving.

CHAPTER 2: MORNING WARMTH

Almond Banana Millet Mash

Time: 3 hours 20 minutes
Serving Size: 2 bowls
Prep Time: 10 minutes
Cook Time: 3 hours 10 minutes

Each Serving Has:
Calories: 305, Carbohydrates: 40g, Saturated Fat: 1g, Protein: 9g, Fat: 11g, Sodium: 55mg, Potassium: 430mg, Fiber: 6g, Sugar: 7g, Vitamin C: 4mg, Calcium: 85mg, Iron: 2.1mg

Ingredients:
- 1/2 cup [90g] uncooked millet, rinsed
- 1 1/2 cups [355ml] unsweetened almond milk
- 1/2 cup [120ml] water
- 1 ripe banana, mashed
- 2 tbsp almond butter
- 1 tbsp ground flaxseed
- 1 tbsp maple syrup
- 1/2 tsp ground cinnamon
- 1/4 tsp sea salt
- 1 tbsp sliced almonds
- 1 tbsp unsweetened shredded coconut

Directions:
1. Add the rinsed millet to the slow cooker along with the almond milk and water.
2. Stir in the mashed banana, almond butter, ground flaxseed, maple syrup, cinnamon, and sea salt.
3. Mix thoroughly to combine all ingredients evenly.
4. Cover and cook on low for 3 hours and 10 minutes until the millet is tender and the texture is creamy.
5. Stir the mixture well to ensure the banana and almond butter are fully incorporated.
6. Sprinkle with sliced almonds and shredded coconut before serving.

Spiced Pumpkin Amaranth Porridge

Time: 3 hours 20 minutes
Serving Size: 2 bowls
Prep Time: 10 minutes
Cook Time: 3 hours 10 minutes

Each Serving Has:
Calories: 300, Carbohydrates: 41g, Saturated Fat: 2g, Protein: 9g, Fat: 10g, Sodium: 80mg, Potassium: 420mg, Fiber: 7g, Sugar: 6g, Vitamin C: 3mg, Calcium: 70mg, Iron: 3mg

Ingredients:
- 1/2 cup [96g] amaranth, rinsed
- 1 1/2 cups [355ml] unsweetened soy milk
- 1/2 cup [120ml] water
- 1/2 cup [120g] unsweetened canned pumpkin purée
- 1 tbsp chia seeds
- 1 tbsp maple syrup
- 1/2 tsp pumpkin pie spice
- 1/4 tsp sea salt
- 2 tbsp chopped walnuts
- 2 tbsp dried cranberries

Directions:
1. Add the rinsed amaranth, soy milk, and water to the slow cooker.
2. Stir in the pumpkin purée, chia seeds, maple syrup, pumpkin pie spice, and sea salt.
3. Mix thoroughly to ensure all ingredients are well blended.
4. Cover and cook on low for 3 hours and 10 minutes until the amaranth is tender and the porridge is creamy.
5. Stir the mixture once more to distribute the pumpkin and spices evenly.
6. Top with chopped walnuts and dried cranberries before serving.

Golden Turmeric Oats

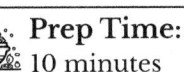

Time: 3 hours 15 minutes
Serving Size: 2 bowls
Prep Time: 10 minutes
Cook Time: 3 hours 5 minutes

Each Serving Has:
Calories: 285, Carbohydrates: 40g, Saturated Fat: 1.5g, Protein: 8g, Fat: 9g, Sodium: 70mg, Potassium: 390mg, Fiber: 6g, Sugar: 5g, Vitamin C: 1mg, Calcium: 95mg, Iron: 2.3mg

Ingredients:
- 1/2 cup [40g] rolled oats
- 1 1/2 cups [355ml] unsweetened cashew milk
- 1/2 cup [120ml] water
- 1 tbsp ground flaxseed
- 1 tbsp maple syrup
- 1/2 tsp ground turmeric
- 1/4 tsp ground cinnamon
- 1/4 tsp ground ginger
- 1/4 tsp sea salt
- 1/8 tsp black pepper
- 1 tbsp chopped pistachios
- 1 tbsp unsweetened coconut flakes

Directions:
1. Add the rolled oats, cashew milk, and water to the slow cooker.
2. Stir in the ground flaxseed, maple syrup, turmeric, cinnamon, ginger, sea salt, and black pepper.
3. Mix thoroughly until the spices are fully incorporated.
4. Cover and cook on low for 3 hours and 5 minutes until the oats are soft and creamy.
5. Stir well to blend the flavors evenly and ensure a golden color throughout.
6. Top with chopped pistachios and coconut flakes before serving.

Blueberry Lemon Breakfast Quinoa

Time: 3 hours 15 minutes
Serving Size: 2 bowls
Prep Time: 10 minutes
Cook Time: 3 hours 5 minutes

Each Serving Has:
Calories: 295, Carbohydrates: 39g, Saturated Fat: 1g, Protein: 9g, Fat: 9g, Sodium: 60mg, Potassium: 370mg, Fiber: 5g, Sugar: 7g, Vitamin C: 6mg, Calcium: 80mg, Iron: 2.5mg

Ingredients:
- 1/2 cup [85g] uncooked quinoa, rinsed
- 1 1/2 cups [355ml] unsweetened oat milk
- 1/2 cup [120ml] water
- 1 tbsp maple syrup
- 1 tbsp chia seeds
- 1/2 tsp finely grated lemon zest
- 1/2 tsp vanilla extract
- 1/4 tsp ground cinnamon
- 1/4 tsp sea salt
- 1/2 cup [75g] fresh or frozen blueberries
- 2 tbsp chopped cashews

Directions:
1. Add the rinsed quinoa, oat milk, and water to the slow cooker.
2. Stir in the maple syrup, chia seeds, lemon zest, vanilla extract, cinnamon, and sea salt.
3. Mix thoroughly to combine the flavors evenly.
4. Gently fold in the blueberries, distributing them throughout the mixture.
5. Cover and cook on low for 3 hours and 5 minutes until the quinoa is tender and the porridge has thickened.
6. Stir the porridge once to blend the cooked blueberries throughout.
7. Sprinkle with chopped cashews before serving.

Peanut Butter Cacao Oats

Time: 3 hours 15 minutes
Serving Size: 2 bowls
Prep Time: 10 minutes
Cook Time: 3 hours 5 minutes

Each Serving Has:
Calories: 320, Carbohydrates: 38g, Saturated Fat: 2g, Protein: 10g, Fat: 13g, Sodium: 75mg, Potassium: 410mg, Fiber: 7g, Sugar: 6g, Vitamin C: 0mg, Calcium: 60mg, Iron: 2.2mg

Ingredients:
- 1/2 cup [40g] rolled oats
- 1 1/2 cups [355ml] unsweetened almond milk
- 1/2 cup [120ml] water
- 2 tbsp natural peanut butter
- 1 tbsp maple syrup
- 1 tbsp unsweetened cacao powder
- 1 tbsp ground flaxseed
- 1/2 tsp vanilla extract
- 1/4 tsp sea salt
- 1 tbsp crushed peanuts
- 1 tbsp cacao nibs

Directions:
1. Add the rolled oats to the slow cooker along with the almond milk and water.
2. Stir in the peanut butter, maple syrup, cacao powder, ground flaxseed, vanilla extract, and sea salt.
3. Mix well to ensure all ingredients are evenly combined.
4. Cover and cook on low for 3 hours and 5 minutes until the oats are creamy and the flavors are infused.
5. Stir thoroughly to distribute the peanut butter and cacao evenly.
6. Top with crushed peanuts and cacao nibs before serving.

Coconut Date Breakfast Rice

Time: 3 hours 20 minutes
Serving Size: 2 bowls
Prep Time: 10 minutes
Cook Time: 3 hours 10 minutes

Each Serving Has:
Calories: 310, Carbohydrates: 45g, Saturated Fat: 4g, Protein: 6g, Fat: 10g, Sodium: 50mg, Potassium: 330mg, Fiber: 4g, Sugar: 9g, Vitamin C: 0mg, Calcium: 40mg, Iron: 1.8mg

Ingredients:
- 1/2 cup [97g] jasmine rice, rinsed
- 1 1/2 cups [355ml] unsweetened coconut milk
- 1/2 cup [120ml] water
- 4 Medjool dates, pitted and chopped
- 2 tbsp unsweetened shredded coconut
- 1 tbsp maple syrup
- 1/2 tsp ground cardamom
- 1/4 tsp ground cinnamon
- 1/4 tsp sea salt
- 1 tbsp chopped almonds
- 1 tbsp toasted coconut flakes

Directions:
1. Add the rinsed jasmine rice, coconut milk, and water to the slow cooker.
2. Stir in the chopped dates, shredded coconut, maple syrup, cardamom, cinnamon, and sea salt.
3. Mix thoroughly to distribute the ingredients evenly.
4. Cover and cook on low for 3 hours and 10 minutes until the rice is tender and the mixture is creamy.
5. Stir gently to incorporate the softened dates and blend the flavors.
6. Top with chopped almonds and toasted coconut flakes before serving.

Warm Fig & Hazelnut Farro

Time: 3 hours 25 minutes
Serving Size: 2 bowls
Prep Time: 10 minutes
Cook Time: 3 hours 15 minutes

Each Serving Has:
Calories: 315, Carbohydrates: 42g, Saturated Fat: 1g, Protein: 9g, Fat: 11g, Sodium: 60mg, Potassium: 390mg, Fiber: 5g, Sugar: 8g, Vitamin C: 1mg, Calcium: 55mg, Iron: 2.6mg

Ingredients:
- 1/2 cup [95g] pearled farro, rinsed
- 1 1/2 cups [355ml] unsweetened almond milk
- 1/2 cup [120ml] water
- 4 dried figs, chopped
- 1 tbsp maple syrup
- 1 tbsp ground flaxseed
- 1/2 tsp ground cinnamon
- 1/4 tsp sea salt
- 1/4 tsp ground nutmeg
- 2 tbsp chopped hazelnuts
- 1 tbsp chopped dried apricots

Directions:
1. Add the rinsed farro, almond milk, and water to the slow cooker.
2. Stir in the chopped dried figs, maple syrup, ground flaxseed, cinnamon, sea salt, and nutmeg.
3. Mix well to combine all ingredients thoroughly.
4. Cover and cook on low for 3 hours and 15 minutes until the farro is tender and creamy.
5. Stir the mixture to blend the softened figs and spices evenly throughout.
6. Top with chopped hazelnuts and chopped dried apricots before serving.

Vanilla Pear Millet Bowl

Time: 3 hours 20 minutes
Serving Size: 2 bowls
Prep Time: 10 minutes
Cook Time: 3 hours 10 minutes

Each Serving Has:
Calories: 300, Carbohydrates: 43g, Saturated Fat: 1.5g, Protein: 8g, Fat: 9g, Sodium: 55mg, Potassium: 410mg, Fiber: 6g, Sugar: 7g, Vitamin C: 5mg, Calcium: 70mg, Iron: 2.2mg

Ingredients:
- 1/2 cup [90g] uncooked millet, rinsed
- 1 1/2 cups [355ml] unsweetened oat milk
- 1/2 cup [120ml] water
- 1 ripe pear, peeled and diced
- 1 tbsp ground flaxseed
- 1 tbsp maple syrup
- 1/2 tsp vanilla extract
- 1/2 tsp ground cinnamon
- 1/4 tsp ground cardamom
- 1/4 tsp sea salt
- 1 tbsp chopped pecans
- 1 tbsp hemp seeds

Directions:
1. Add the rinsed millet, oat milk, and water to the slow cooker.
2. Stir in the diced pear, ground flaxseed, maple syrup, vanilla extract, cinnamon, cardamom, and sea salt.
3. Mix well to distribute the ingredients evenly.
4. Cover and cook on low for 3 hours and 10 minutes until the millet is soft and creamy.
5. Stir thoroughly to blend the pear and spices into the porridge.
6. Top with chopped pecans and hemp seeds before serving.

Strawberry Basil Chia Pudding

Time: 3 hours 10 minutes	Serving Size: 2 bowls
Prep Time: 10 minutes	Cook Time: 3 hours

Each Serving Has:
Calories: 280, Carbohydrates: 34g, Saturated Fat: 1g, Protein: 8g, Fat: 11g, Sodium: 40mg, Potassium: 370mg, Fiber: 9g, Sugar: 10g, Vitamin C: 42mg, Calcium: 180mg, Iron: 2.4mg

Ingredients:
- 1/4 cup [43g] chia seeds
- 1 1/2 cups [355ml] unsweetened almond milk
- 1/2 cup [120ml] water
- 1 cup [150g] fresh strawberries, chopped (plus extra for garnish)
- 1 tbsp maple syrup
- 1 tsp vanilla extract
- 1/4 tsp sea salt
- 1 tbsp finely chopped fresh basil
- 1 tbsp sliced almonds

Directions:
1. Add the chia seeds to the slow cooker along with the almond milk and water.
2. Stir in the chopped strawberries, maple syrup, vanilla extract, and sea salt until combined.
3. Add the chopped fresh basil and stir gently to distribute the flavor evenly.
4. Cover and cook on low for 3 hours, allowing the chia seeds to absorb the liquid and thicken.
5. Stir the mixture well to ensure an even texture and full incorporation of the fruit.
6. Top with sliced almonds and extra chopped strawberries before serving.

Banana Bread Breakfast Oats

Time: 3 hours 15 minutes	Serving Size: 2 bowls
Prep Time: 10 minutes	Cook Time: 3 hours 5 minutes

Each Serving Has:
Calories: 310, Carbohydrates: 42g, Saturated Fat: 1.5g, Protein: 8g, Fat: 9g, Sodium: 65mg, Potassium: 430mg, Fiber: 6g, Sugar: 10g, Vitamin C: 3mg, Calcium: 70mg, Iron: 2.4mg

Ingredients:
- 1/2 cup [40g] rolled oats
- 1 1/2 cups [355ml] unsweetened oat milk
- 1/2 cup [120ml] water
- 1 ripe banana, mashed (plus a few extra slices for garnish)
- 1 tbsp ground flaxseed
- 1 tbsp maple syrup
- 1/2 tsp ground cinnamon
- 1/4 tsp ground nutmeg
- 1/4 tsp sea salt
- 1 tbsp chopped walnuts

Directions:
1. Add the rolled oats, oat milk, and water to the slow cooker.
2. Stir in the mashed banana, ground flaxseed, maple syrup, cinnamon, nutmeg, and sea salt.
3. Mix well until all ingredients are evenly distributed.
4. Cover and cook on low for 3 hours and 5 minutes until the oats are tender and creamy.
5. Stir the mixture thoroughly to blend the banana and spices into the oats.
6. Top with chopped walnuts and a few slices of fresh banana before serving.

Apple Pie Cauliflower Bowl

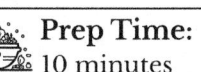

⏲ Time: 3 hours 15 minutes	🍴 Serving Size: 2 bowls
🥣 Prep Time: 10 minutes	🍲 Cook Time: 3 hours 5 minutes

Each Serving Has:
Calories: 270, Carbohydrates: 36g, Saturated Fat: 2g, Protein: 7g, Fat: 9g, Sodium: 55mg, Potassium: 460mg, Fiber: 6g, Sugar: 11g, Vitamin C: 50mg, Calcium: 60mg, Iron: 2.3mg

Ingredients:
- 2 cups [200g] riced cauliflower
- 1 1/2 cups [355ml] unsweetened almond milk
- 1/2 cup [120ml] water
- 1 apple, peeled and finely chopped
- 2 tbsp rolled oats
- 1 tbsp maple syrup
- 1 tbsp almond butter
- 1/2 tsp ground cinnamon
- 1/4 tsp ground nutmeg
- 1/4 tsp sea salt
- 1 tbsp chopped walnuts
- 1 tbsp raisins

Directions:
1. Add the riced cauliflower, almond milk, and water to the slow cooker.
2. Stir in the chopped apple, rolled oats, maple syrup, almond butter, cinnamon, nutmeg, and sea salt.
3. Mix well to combine all ingredients evenly.
4. Cover and cook on low for 3 hours and 5 minutes until the cauliflower and apples are tender and the mixture is thickened.
5. Stir thoroughly to distribute the almond butter and spices throughout the bowl.
6. Top with chopped walnuts and raisins before serving.

Tropical Mango Quinoa Mash

⏲ Time: 3 hours 15 minutes	🍴 Serving Size: 2 bowls
🥣 Prep Time: 10 minutes	🍲 Cook Time: 3 hours 5 minutes

Each Serving Has:
Calories: 305, Carbohydrates: 44g, Saturated Fat: 2g, Protein: 9g, Fat: 8g, Sodium: 50mg, Potassium: 420mg, Fiber: 5g, Sugar: 10g, Vitamin C: 35mg, Calcium: 60mg, Iron: 2.7mg

Ingredients:
- 1/2 cup [85g] uncooked quinoa, rinsed
- 1 1/2 cups [355ml] unsweetened coconut milk
- 1/2 cup [120ml] water
- 1 cup [165g] fresh or frozen mango, diced (plus a few extra pieces for garnish)
- 1 tbsp shredded unsweetened coconut
- 1 tbsp chia seeds
- 1 tbsp maple syrup
- 1/2 tsp ground ginger
- 1/4 tsp sea salt
- 1 tbsp chopped macadamia nuts

Directions:
1. Add the rinsed quinoa, coconut milk, and water to the slow cooker.
2. Stir in the diced mango, shredded coconut, chia seeds, maple syrup, ginger, and sea salt.
3. Mix well to combine all ingredients evenly.
4. Cover and cook on low for 3 hours and 5 minutes until the quinoa is soft and the texture becomes creamy.
5. Stir the mixture to distribute the fruit and spices evenly throughout the mash.
6. Top with chopped macadamia nuts and a few pieces of diced mango before serving.

CHAPTER 2: MORNING WARMTH

Lavender Vanilla Barley Bowl

⏰ **Time:** 3 hours 20 minutes	🍽 **Serving Size:** 2 bowls
🍚 **Prep Time:** 10 minutes	🍲 **Cook Time:** 3 hours 10 minutes

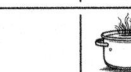

Each Serving Has:
Calories: 290, Carbohydrates: 41g, Saturated Fat: 1g, Protein: 7g, Fat: 8g, Sodium: 45mg, Potassium: 350mg, Fiber: 6g, Sugar: 6g, Vitamin C: 0mg, Calcium: 60mg, Iron: 2.5mg

Ingredients:
- 1/2 cup [95g] pearl barley, rinsed
- 1 1/2 cups [355ml] unsweetened almond milk
- 1/2 cup [120ml] water
- 1 tbsp maple syrup
- 1/2 tsp pure vanilla extract
- 1/2 tsp dried culinary lavender
- 1 tbsp ground flaxseed
- 1/4 tsp sea salt
- 1 tbsp chopped pistachios
- 1 tbsp dried cranberries

Directions:
1. Add the rinsed pearl barley, almond milk, and water to the slow cooker.
2. Stir in the maple syrup, vanilla extract, dried lavender, ground flaxseed, and sea salt.
3. Mix well to distribute all ingredients evenly.
4. Cover and cook on low for 3 hours and 10 minutes until the barley is tender and the mixture thickens.
5. Stir the porridge gently to blend the lavender and vanilla flavors thoroughly.
6. Top with chopped pistachios and dried cranberries before serving.

Sweet Potato Pie Oats

⏰ **Time:** 3 hours 15 minutes	🍽 **Serving Size:** 2 bowls
🍚 **Prep Time:** 10 minutes	🍲 **Cook Time:** 3 hours 5 minutes

Each Serving Has:
Calories: 320, Carbohydrates: 46g, Saturated Fat: 1.5g, Protein: 8g, Fat: 9g, Sodium: 60mg, Potassium: 480mg, Fiber: 7g, Sugar: 9g, Vitamin C: 6mg, Calcium: 75mg, Iron: 2.8mg

Ingredients:
- 1/2 cup [40g] rolled oats
- 1 1/2 cups [355ml] unsweetened soy milk
- 1/2 cup [120ml] water
- 1/2 cup [120g] cooked mashed sweet potato
- 1 tbsp ground flaxseed
- 1 tbsp maple syrup
- 1/2 tsp ground cinnamon
- 1/4 tsp ground nutmeg
- 1/4 tsp sea salt
- 1/4 tsp vanilla extract
- 1 tbsp chopped pecans
- 1 tbsp dried currants

Directions:
1. Add the rolled oats, soy milk, and water to the slow cooker.
2. Stir in the mashed sweet potato, ground flaxseed, maple syrup, cinnamon, nutmeg, sea salt, and vanilla extract.
3. Mix thoroughly until all ingredients are evenly combined.
4. Cover and cook on low for 3 hours and 5 minutes until the oats are creamy and the flavors have blended.
5. Stir the mixture well to incorporate the sweet potato and spices fully.
6. Top with chopped pecans and dried currants before serving.

Chapter 3: Small Bites

Smoky Maple Chickpeas

Time: 3 hours 10 minutes	Serving Size: 2 cups
Prep Time: 10 minutes	Cook Time: 3 hours

Each Serving Has:
Calories: 295, Carbohydrates: 38g, Saturated Fat: 0.5g, Protein: 13g, Fat: 7g, Sodium: 290mg, Potassium: 470mg, Fiber: 10g, Sugar: 9g, Vitamin C: 2mg, Calcium: 60mg, Iron: 3.1mg

Ingredients:
- 1 1/2 cups [255g] cooked chickpeas
- 1/2 cup [120ml] low-sodium vegetable broth
- 1 tbsp maple syrup
- 1 tbsp tomato paste (no salt added)
- 1/2 tsp smoked paprika
- 1/4 tsp ground cumin
- 1/4 tsp garlic powder
- 1/4 tsp onion powder
- 1/4 tsp sea salt
- 1/8 tsp black pepper
- 1 tbsp chopped fresh parsley

Directions:
1. Add the cooked chickpeas to the slow cooker along with the vegetable broth.
2. Stir in the maple syrup, tomato paste, smoked paprika, cumin, garlic powder, onion powder, sea salt, and black pepper.
3. Mix thoroughly to coat the chickpeas in the smoky-sweet sauce.
4. Cover and cook on low for 3 hours until the flavors meld and the sauce thickens.
5. Stir occasionally during cooking to prevent sticking and ensure even coating.
6. Garnish with chopped fresh parsley before serving.

Slow-Roasted Spiced Nuts

Time: 3 hours 10 minutes
Serving Size: 2 small bowls
Prep Time: 10 minutes
Cook Time: 3 hours

Each Serving Has:
Calories: 310, Carbohydrates: 11g, Saturated Fat: 2g, Protein: 9g, Fat: 26g, Sodium: 150mg, Potassium: 290mg, Fiber: 4g, Sugar: 4g, Vitamin C: 0mg, Calcium: 50mg, Iron: 2.2mg

Ingredients:
- 1/2 cup [60g] raw almonds
- 1/4 cup [30g] raw cashews
- 1/4 cup [30g] raw walnuts
- 1 tbsp maple syrup
- 1 tbsp tamari (or low-sodium soy sauce)
- 1/2 tsp smoked paprika
- 1/4 tsp ground cumin
- 1/4 tsp garlic powder
- 1/4 tsp onion powder
- 1/8 tsp cayenne pepper (optional)
- 1/4 tsp sea salt

Directions:
1. Add the almonds, cashews, and walnuts to the slow cooker in an even layer.
2. In a small bowl, mix the maple syrup, tamari, smoked paprika, cumin, garlic powder, onion powder, cayenne pepper (if using), and sea salt.
3. Pour the spice mixture over the nuts and stir well to coat them evenly.
4. Cover and cook on low for 3 hours, stirring every 30 minutes to prevent sticking and ensure even roasting.
5. Once the nuts are golden and fragrant, turn off the heat and let them cool slightly in the slow cooker.
6. Store leftovers in an airtight container once fully cooled.

Buffalo Cauliflower Bites

Time: 3 hours 10 minutes
Serving Size: 2 cups
Prep Time: 10 minutes
Cook Time: 3 hours

Each Serving Has:
Calories: 165, Carbohydrates: 20g, Saturated Fat: 0.5g, Protein: 5g, Fat: 7g, Sodium: 290mg, Potassium: 470mg, Fiber: 5g, Sugar: 4g, Vitamin C: 68mg, Calcium: 45mg, Iron: 1.3mg

Ingredients:
- 3 cups [300g] cauliflower florets
- 1/4 cup [60ml] low-sodium vegetable broth
- 2 tbsp hot sauce (vinegar-based, plant-based compliant)
- 1 tbsp olive oil
- 1 tbsp apple cider vinegar
- 1/2 tsp garlic powder
- 1/2 tsp onion powder
- 1/4 tsp smoked paprika
- 1/4 tsp sea salt
- 1 tbsp chopped fresh parsley

Directions:
1. Add the cauliflower florets to the slow cooker in an even layer.
2. In a small bowl, whisk together the vegetable broth, hot sauce, olive oil, apple cider vinegar, garlic powder, onion powder, smoked paprika, and sea salt.
3. Pour the mixture over the cauliflower and stir to coat the pieces evenly.
4. Cover and cook on low for 3 hours until the cauliflower is tender but not mushy.
5. Stir once or twice during cooking to ensure even flavor distribution.
6. Sprinkle with chopped fresh parsley before serving.

Stuffed Bell Pepper Scoops

Time: 3 hours 10 minutes
Serving Size: 2 plates
Prep Time: 10 minutes
Cook Time: 3 hours

Each Serving Has:
Calories: 275, Carbohydrates: 35g, Saturated Fat: 0.5g, Protein: 9g, Fat: 10g, Sodium: 210mg, Potassium: 560mg, Fiber: 8g, Sugar: 7g, Vitamin C: 110mg, Calcium: 50mg, Iron: 2.5mg

Ingredients:
- 2 large bell peppers, halved and seeds removed
- 1/2 cup [90g] cooked brown rice
- 1/2 cup [85g] cooked black beans
- 1/4 cup [40g] corn kernels (fresh or frozen)
- 1/4 cup [60ml] low-sodium tomato sauce
- 1 tbsp chopped fresh cilantro
- 1 tbsp nutritional yeast
- 1/2 tsp ground cumin
- 1/4 tsp smoked paprika
- 1/4 tsp garlic powder
- 1/4 tsp sea salt
- 1 tbsp diced avocado
- 1 tbsp chopped green onions

Directions:
1. Place the halved bell peppers into the bottom of the slow cooker, cut side up.
2. In a bowl, combine the cooked brown rice, black beans, corn, tomato sauce, cilantro, nutritional yeast, cumin, smoked paprika, garlic powder, and sea salt.
3. Stir the mixture well to blend the flavors and coat the ingredients evenly.
4. Spoon the filling intoEach bell pepper half, packing it gently.
5. Cover and cook on low for 3 hours until the peppers are tender and the filling is heated through.
6. Once done, use a spoon to liftEach pepper half onto a plate carefully.
7. Top with diced avocado and chopped green onions before serving.

Ginger-Garlic Edamame

Time: 3 hours 10 minutes
Serving Size: 2 bowls
Prep Time: 10 minutes
Cook Time: 3 hours

Each Serving Has:
Calories: 230, Carbohydrates: 17g, Saturated Fat: 0.5g, Protein: 16g, Fat: 10g, Sodium: 240mg, Potassium: 460mg, Fiber: 6g, Sugar: 2g, Vitamin C: 3mg, Calcium: 60mg, Iron: 3mg

Ingredients:
- 2 cups [280g] shelled edamame (fresh or frozen)
- 1/4 cup [60ml] low-sodium vegetable broth
- 1 tbsp tamari (or low-sodium soy sauce)
- 1 tbsp sesame oil
- 1 tbsp grated fresh ginger
- 2 cloves garlic, minced
- 1/4 tsp sea salt
- 1/4 tsp crushed red pepper flakes (optional)
- 1 tbsp chopped scallions
- 1 tsp sesame seeds

Directions:
1. Add the shelled edamame to the slow cooker along with the vegetable broth.
2. Stir in the tamari, sesame oil, grated ginger, minced garlic, sea salt, and red pepper flakes (if using).
3. Mix thoroughly to coat the edamame with the flavorful sauce.
4. Cover and cook on low for 3 hours until the edamame is tender and infused with seasoning.
5. Stir once during cooking to ensure even flavor distribution.
6. Garnish with chopped scallions and sesame seeds before serving.

CHAPTER 3: SMALL BITES

Slow-Cooked Salsa Dip

⏰ **Time:** 3 hours 10 minutes	🍽 **Serving Size:** 2 bowls
🍲 **Prep Time:** 10 minutes	🍳 **Cook Time:** 3 hours

Each Serving Has:
Calories: 190, Carbohydrates: 25g, Saturated Fat: 0.5g, Protein: 6g, Fat: 7g, Sodium: 300mg, Potassium: 560mg, Fiber: 6g, Sugar: 9g, Vitamin C: 18mg, Calcium: 50mg, Iron: 2.4mg

Ingredients:
- 1 cup [240g] canned diced tomatoes (no salt added)
- 1/2 cup [85g] cooked black beans
- 1/2 cup [75g] corn kernels (fresh or frozen)
- 1/4 cup [40g] finely chopped red onion
- 1 clove garlic, minced
- 1 tbsp lime juice
- 1 tbsp chopped fresh cilantro
- 1/2 tsp ground cumin
- 1/4 tsp chili powder
- 1/4 tsp sea salt
- 1 tbsp diced avocado
- 1 tbsp chopped green onions

Directions:
1. Add the diced tomatoes, black beans, and corn to the slow cooker.
2. Stir in the chopped red onion, minced garlic, lime juice, chopped cilantro, cumin, chili powder, and sea salt.
3. Mix thoroughly to combine all the ingredients evenly.
4. Cover and cook on low for 3 hours, allowing the flavors to meld and the mixture to thicken.
5. Stir once during cooking to prevent sticking and maintain consistency.
6. Top with diced avocado and chopped green onions before serving.

Herb & Olive Bean Medley

⏰ **Time:** 3 hours 10 minutes	🍽 **Serving Size:** 2 bowls
🍲 **Prep Time:** 10 minutes	🍳 **Cook Time:** 3 hours

Each Serving Has:
Calories: 280, Carbohydrates: 29g, Saturated Fat: 1g, Protein: 13g, Fat: 12g, Sodium: 330mg, Potassium: 520mg, Fiber: 9g, Sugar: 3g, Vitamin C: 4mg, Calcium: 70mg, Iron: 3.5mg

Ingredients:
- 1/2 cup [85g] cooked cannellini beans
- 1/2 cup [85g] cooked chickpeas
- 1/2 cup [85g] cooked kidney beans
- 1/4 cup [40g] chopped green olives
- 1/4 cup [60ml] low-sodium vegetable broth
- 1 tbsp extra virgin olive oil
- 1 tbsp chopped fresh parsley
- 1/2 tsp dried oregano
- 1/2 tsp dried thyme
- 1/4 tsp garlic powder
- 1/4 tsp black pepper
- 1/4 tsp sea salt
- 1 tbsp chopped sun-dried tomatoes (oil-free)

Directions:
1. Add the cannellini beans, chickpeas, and kidney beans to the slow cooker.
2. Stir in the chopped green olives, vegetable broth, and olive oil.
3. Add the chopped parsley, oregano, thyme, garlic powder, black pepper, and sea salt.
4. Mix thoroughly to coat the beans with herbs and oil evenly.
5. Cover and cook on low for 3 hours until the flavors meld and the beans are tender.
6. Stir once during cooking to maintain an even texture and prevent sticking.
7. Garnish with chopped sun-dried tomatoes before serving.

Sweet Potato Tot Cups

⏱ Time: 3 hours 10 minutes	🍽 Serving Size: 2 cups
🥣 Prep Time: 10 minutes	🍲 Cook Time: 3 hours

Each Serving Has:
Calories: 260, Carbohydrates: 36g, Saturated Fat: 0.5g, Protein: 6g, Fat: 9g, Sodium: 210mg, Potassium: 540mg, Fiber: 5g, Sugar: 8g, Vitamin C: 14mg, Calcium: 40mg, Iron: 1.7mg

Ingredients:
- 1 1/2 cups [270g] grated sweet potato
- 1/2 cup [75g] cooked quinoa
- 1 tbsp ground flaxseed
- 2 tbsp finely chopped onion
- 1 tbsp nutritional yeast
- 1/2 tsp garlic powder
- 1/2 tsp smoked paprika
- 1/4 tsp sea salt
- 1/4 tsp black pepper
- 1 tbsp olive oil (plus extra for greasing)
- 1 tbsp chopped chives

Directions:
1. In a mixing bowl, combine grated sweet potato, cooked quinoa, and ground flaxseed.
2. Add chopped onion, nutritional yeast, garlic powder, smoked paprika, sea salt, and black pepper.
3. Stir the mixture until everything is evenly combined.
4. Lightly oil silicone muffin liners and press the mixture intoEach cup, forming a small well.
5. Place the liners into the slow cooker and drizzle the olive oil over the tops.
6. Cover and cook on low for 3 hours until the cups are firm and lightly browned on the edges.
7. Remove from the slow cooker and let them cool slightly before unmolding.
8. Garnish with chopped chives before serving.

Sticky Sesame Mushrooms

⏱ Time: 3 hours 10 minutes	🍽 Serving Size: 2 bowls
🥣 Prep Time: 10 minutes	🍲 Cook Time: 3 hours

Each Serving Has:
Calories: 220, Carbohydrates: 19g, Saturated Fat: 1g, Protein: 7g, Fat: 13g, Sodium: 380mg, Potassium: 510mg, Fiber: 3g, Sugar: 8g, Vitamin C: 3mg, Calcium: 40mg, Iron: 1.9mg

Ingredients:
- 3 cups [210g] cremini mushrooms, halved
- 2 tbsp low-sodium soy sauce (or tamari)
- 1 tbsp maple syrup
- 1 tbsp sesame oil
- 1 tbsp rice vinegar
- 1 clove garlic, minced
- 1/2 tsp grated fresh ginger
- 1/2 tsp cornstarch
- 1 tbsp water
- 1 tsp sesame seeds
- 1 tbsp chopped scallions

Directions:
1. Add the halved mushrooms to the slow cooker.
2. In a small bowl, mix the soy sauce, maple syrup, sesame oil, rice vinegar, minced garlic, and grated ginger.
3. Pour the sauce over the mushrooms and stir to coat evenly.
4. Cover and cook on low for 3 hours, allowing the mushrooms to absorb the flavors.
5. Mix the cornstarch with water in the last 10 minutes of cooking and stir it into the slow cooker.
6. Let the sauce thicken slightly while the mushrooms continue to cook.
7. Top the mushrooms with sesame seeds and chopped scallions before serving.

CHAPTER 3: SMALL BITES ◊ 23

Zesty Lentil Poppers

Time: 3 hours 10 minutes	Serving Size: 2 bowls
Prep Time: 10 minutes	Cook Time: 3 hours

Each Serving Has:
Calories: 260, Carbohydrates: 32g, Saturated Fat: 0.5g, Protein: 12g, Fat: 8g, Sodium: 240mg, Potassium: 540mg, Fiber: 10g, Sugar: 3g, Vitamin C: 2mg, Calcium: 45mg, Iron: 3.4mg

Ingredients:
- 1 cup [200g] cooked green lentils
- 1/2 cup [75g] grated carrot
- 1/4 cup [40g] finely chopped red bell pepper
- 2 tbsp ground flaxseed
- 2 tbsp rolled oats
- 1 tbsp lemon juice
- 1 tbsp chopped fresh parsley
- 1/2 tsp ground cumin
- 1/2 tsp garlic powder
- 1/4 tsp smoked paprika
- 1/4 tsp sea salt
- 1 tbsp olive oil

Directions:
1. Add the cooked lentils, grated carrot, and chopped bell pepper to a mixing bowl.
2. Stir in the ground flaxseed, rolled oats, lemon juice, and chopped parsley. Season the mixture with cumin, garlic powder, smoked paprika, and sea salt.
3. Mix until a thick dough forms and holds shape when pressed.
4. Shape the mixture into small poppers about 1 inch wide.
5. Lightly brushEach popper with olive oil to help with browning.
6. Place the poppers in a single layer in the slow cooker.
7. Cover and cook on low for 3 hours until firm and slightly crisp.
8. Let the poppers cool slightly before serving.

Jalapeño Corn Dip

Time: 3 hours 10 minutes	Serving Size: 2 bowls
Prep Time: 10 minutes	Cook Time: 3 hours

Each Serving Has:
Calories: 240, Carbohydrates: 29g, Saturated Fat: 1g, Protein: 7g, Fat: 10g, Sodium: 260mg, Potassium: 410mg, Fiber: 5g, Sugar: 6g, Vitamin C: 18mg, Calcium: 40mg, Iron: 1.6mg

Ingredients:
- 1 1/2 cups [240g] corn kernels (fresh or frozen)
- 1/4 cup [40g] finely diced red bell pepper
- 1 small jalapeño, seeded and minced
- 1/4 cup [60ml] unsweetened plain plant-based yogurt
- 1 tbsp nutritional yeast
- 1 tbsp lime juice
- 1 tbsp chopped fresh cilantro
- 1/2 tsp garlic powder
- 1/4 tsp smoked paprika
- 1/4 tsp sea salt
- 1/4 tsp black pepper
- 1 tbsp chopped green onions

Directions:
Add the corn kernels, diced red bell pepper, and minced jalapeño to the slow cooker.
Stir in the plant-based yogurt, nutritional yeast, and lime juice.
Add the chopped cilantro, garlic powder, smoked paprika, sea salt, and black pepper. Mix thoroughly until all ingredients are well combined.
Cover and cook on low for 3 hours, stirring once halfway through.
Garnish with the chopped green onions before serving.

Vegan Spinach Artichoke Dip

Time: 3 hours 10 minutes		Serving Size: 2 bowls	
Prep Time: 10 minutes		Cook Time: 3 hours	

Each Serving Has:

Calories: 250, Carbohydrates: 18g, Saturated Fat: 1g, Protein: 9g, Fat: 16g, Sodium: 320mg, Potassium: 540mg, Fiber: 5g, Sugar: 3g, Vitamin C: 12mg, Calcium: 80mg, Iron: 2.7mg

Ingredients:
- 1 cup [150g] canned artichoke hearts, chopped
- 1 cup [30g] fresh spinach, chopped
- 1/2 cup [120ml] unsweetened plant-based cream (or yogurt)
- 1/4 cup [35g] raw cashews, soaked and blended
- 2 tbsp nutritional yeast
- 1 tbsp lemon juice
- 1 clove garlic, minced
- 1/2 tsp onion powder
- 1/4 tsp sea salt
- 1/4 tsp black pepper
- 1 tbsp chopped fresh parsley

Directions:

Add the chopped artichoke hearts and spinach to the slow cooker.
Stir in the plant-based cream, blended cashews, and nutritional yeast.
Add the lemon juice, minced garlic, onion powder, sea salt, and black pepper.
Mix thoroughly until all ingredients are well combined.
Cover and cook on low for 3 hours, stirring once halfway through.
Once heated and creamy, stir the dip again for an even texture.
Garnish with the chopped fresh parsley before serving.

Cashew Carrot Spread

Time: 3 hours 10 minutes		Serving Size: 2 ramekins	
Prep Time: 10 minutes		Cook Time: 3 hours	

Each Serving Has:

Calories: 270, Carbohydrates: 23g, Saturated Fat: 2g, Protein: 9g, Fat: 18g, Sodium: 180mg, Potassium: 490mg, Fiber: 4g, Sugar: 6g, Vitamin C: 5mg, Calcium: 60mg, Iron: 2.1mg

Ingredients:
- 1 cup [130g] chopped carrots
- 1/4 cup [35g] raw cashews, soaked and drained
- 1/4 cup [60ml] unsweetened almond milk (plus extra for thinning, if needed)
- 1 tbsp lemon juice
- 1 tbsp olive oil
- 1 clove garlic, minced
- 1/2 tsp ground cumin
- 1/4 tsp ground coriander
- 1/4 tsp sea salt
- 1/8 tsp black pepper
- 1 tbsp chopped chives

Directions:

1. Add the chopped carrots to the slow cooker with almond milk and olive oil.
2. Stir in the soaked cashews, lemon juice, minced garlic, cumin, coriander, sea salt, and black pepper.
3. Mix thoroughly so all ingredients are coated evenly.
4. Cover and cook on low for 3 hours until carrots are fork-tender.
5. Transfer the mixture to a blender or food processor.
6. Blend until smooth and creamy, adding more almond milk as needed to adjust the consistency.
7. Garnish with the chopped chives before serving.

CHAPTER 3: SMALL BITES

Roasted Red Pepper Hummus

Time: 3 hours 10 minutes
Serving Size: 2 bowls
Prep Time: 10 minutes
Cook Time: 3 hours

Each Serving Has:
Calories: 260, Carbohydrates: 27g, Saturated Fat: 1g, Protein: 10g, Fat: 13g, Sodium: 270mg, Potassium: 430mg, Fiber: 7g, Sugar: 4g, Vitamin C: 36mg, Calcium: 60mg, Iron: 2.8mg

Ingredients:
- 1 cup [165g] cooked chickpeas
- 1/2 cup [75g] chopped roasted red bell pepper
- 2 tbsp tahini
- 1 clove garlic, minced
- 1 tbsp lemon juice
- 1 tbsp olive oil
- 1/4 cup [60ml] water
- 1/2 tsp ground cumin
- 1/4 tsp sea salt
- 1/8 tsp smoked paprika
- 1 tbsp chopped fresh parsley

Directions:
1. Add the cooked chickpeas, roasted bell pepper, tahini, and minced garlic to the slow cooker.
2. Stir in the lemon juice, olive oil, water, cumin, sea salt, and smoked paprika.
3. Mix until all ingredients are well combined.
4. Cover and cook on low for 3 hours to soften and blend flavors.
5. Transfer the mixture to a food processor or blender.
6. Blend until smooth, adding more water as needed to reach the desired consistency.
7. Garnish with the chopped fresh parsley before serving.

Coconut Curry Popcorn Mix

Time: 3 hours 10 minutes
Serving Size: 2 bowls
Prep Time: 10 minutes
Cook Time: 3 hours

Each Serving Has:
Calories: 230, Carbohydrates: 22g, Saturated Fat: 3g, Protein: 5g, Fat: 13g, Sodium: 180mg, Potassium: 190mg, Fiber: 4g, Sugar: 2g, Vitamin C: 0mg, Calcium: 15mg, Iron: 1.2mg

Ingredients:
- 4 cups [32g] air-popped popcorn
- 2 tbsp unsweetened shredded coconut
- 1 tbsp coconut oil, melted
- 1 tbsp maple syrup
- 1/2 tsp curry powder
- 1/4 tsp ground turmeric
- 1/4 tsp sea salt
- 1/8 tsp cayenne pepper (optional)
- 1 tbsp chopped unsweetened dried mango
- 1 tbsp roasted pumpkin seeds

Directions:
1. Add the popcorn and shredded coconut to the slow cooker.
2. In a small bowl, whisk together the melted coconut oil, maple syrup, curry powder, turmeric, sea salt, and cayenne pepper (if using).
3. Pour the seasoned mixture over the popcorn and stir to coat evenly.
4. Cover and cook on low for 3 hours, stirring every 30 minutes.
5. In the last 10 minutes of cooking, stir in the dried mango and pumpkin seeds.
6. Uncover and let the mix cool slightly in the slow cooker until crisp.
7. Once completely cooled, store the popcorn mix in an airtight container.

BBQ Pulled Mushroom Sliders

Time: 3 hours 10 minutes
Serving Size: 2 sliders
Prep Time: 10 minutes
Cook Time: 3 hours

Each Serving Has:
Calories: 290, Carbohydrates: 36g, Saturated Fat: 1g, Protein: 9g, Fat: 11g, Sodium: 370mg, Potassium: 510mg, Fiber: 5g, Sugar: 10g, Vitamin C: 6mg, Calcium: 40mg, Iron: 2.3mg

Ingredients:
- 2 cups [170g] shredded oyster mushrooms
- 1/2 cup [120ml] low-sugar vegan BBQ sauce
- 1 tbsp olive oil
- 1/4 cup [40g] finely chopped red onion
- 1 clove garlic, minced
- 1/2 tsp smoked paprika
- 1/4 tsp sea salt
- 1/4 tsp black pepper
- 2 small whole-grain slider buns
- 2 tbsp shredded lettuce

Directions:
1. Add the shredded oyster mushrooms, chopped onion, and minced garlic to the slow cooker.
2. Stir in the vegan BBQ sauce, olive oil, smoked paprika, sea salt, and black pepper.
3. Mix well to coat the mushrooms evenly in the sauce.
4. Cover and cook on low for 3 hours, stirring once halfway through.
5. Once tender, stir again to shred mushrooms further with a fork.
6. Toast slider buns if desired. Spoon the pulled mushroom mixture onto the buns.
7. Top with the shredded lettuce before serving.

Caramelized Onion Bruschetta

Time: 3 hours 10 minutes
Serving Size: 2 plates
Prep Time: 10 minutes
Cook Time: 3 hours

Each Serving Has:
Calories: 240, Carbohydrates: 34g, Saturated Fat: 1g, Protein: 5g, Fat: 9g, Sodium: 260mg, Potassium: 310mg, Fiber: 4g, Sugar: 8g, Vitamin C: 6mg, Calcium: 35mg, Iron: 1.5mg

Ingredients:
- 2 cups [300g] thinly sliced yellow onions
- 1 tbsp olive oil
- 1 tbsp balsamic vinegar
- 1 tsp maple syrup
- 1/4 tsp sea salt
- 1/4 tsp black pepper
- 1 clove garlic, minced
- 4 slices whole-grain baguette
- 1 tbsp chopped fresh parsley

Directions:
1. Add the sliced onions to the slow cooker along with olive oil and minced garlic.
2. Stir in balsamic vinegar, maple syrup, sea salt, and black pepper.
3. Mix well to coat the onions evenly with the seasoning.
4. Cover and cook on low for 3 hours, stirring once halfway through.
5. Toast the baguette slices just before serving.
6. Spoon the caramelized onions ontoEach slice evenly.
7. Garnish with the chopped fresh parsley before serving.

CHAPTER 3: SMALL BITES

Chapter 4: Cozy Bowls

Rustic Tomato Lentil Soup

🕐	**Time:** 3 hours 15 minutes	🍴	**Serving Size:** 2 bowls
🥣	**Prep Time:** 15 minutes	🍲	**Cook Time:** 3 hours

Each Serving Has:
Calories: 290, Carbohydrates: 38g, Saturated Fat: 0.5g, Protein: 15g, Fat: 6g, Sodium: 350mg, Potassium: 720mg, Fiber: 12g, Sugar: 8g, Vitamin C: 20mg, Calcium: 80mg, Iron: 4.5mg

Ingredients:
- 3/4 cup [150g] dried red lentils, rinsed
- 1 cup [240ml] low-sodium vegetable broth
- 1 cup [240g] canned diced tomatoes (no salt added)
- 1/2 cup [75g] chopped carrots
- 1/2 cup [80g] chopped zucchini
- 1/4 cup [40g] chopped yellow onion
- 2 cloves garlic, minced
- 1 tbsp tomato paste (no salt added)
- 1/2 tsp dried basil
- 1/2 tsp dried thyme
- 1/4 tsp sea salt
- 1/4 tsp black pepper
- 1 tbsp chopped fresh parsley

Directions:
1. Add the rinsed lentils, vegetable broth, and diced tomatoes to the slow cooker.
2. Stir in chopped carrots, zucchini, onion, and minced garlic.
3. Add tomato paste, basil, thyme, sea salt, and pepper.
4. Mix well until all ingredients are combined.
5. Cover and cook on low for 3 hours until lentils are soft.
6. Stir the mixture halfway through to ensure even cooking.
7. Garnish the soup with the chopped fresh parsley before serving.

Sweet Potato Corn Chowder

Time: 3 hours 15 minutes
Serving Size: 2 bowls
Prep Time: 15 minutes
Cook Time: 3 hours

Each Serving Has:
Calories: 310, Carbohydrates: 46g, Saturated Fat: 2g, Protein: 7g, Fat: 10g, Sodium: 340mg, Potassium: 690mg, Fiber: 7g, Sugar: 10g, Vitamin C: 24mg, Calcium: 60mg, Iron: 2.3mg

Ingredients:
- 1 1/2 cups [195g] peeled and diced sweet potato
- 3/4 cup [120g] corn kernels (fresh or frozen)
- 1/2 cup [120ml] unsweetened almond milk
- 1/2 cup [120ml] low-sodium vegetable broth
- 1/4 cup [40g] finely chopped yellow onion
- 1 clove garlic, minced
- 1 tbsp olive oil
- 1/2 tsp dried thyme
- 1/4 tsp smoked paprika
- 1/4 tsp sea salt
- 1/8 tsp black pepper
- 1 tbsp chopped chives

Directions:
1. Add the diced sweet potato, corn kernels, chopped onion, and minced garlic to the slow cooker.
2. Pour in the almond milk and vegetable broth.
3. Stir in the olive oil, thyme, smoked paprika, sea salt, and black pepper.
4. Mix until all ingredients are well combined.
5. Cover and cook on low for 3 hours until vegetables are tender.
6. Use an immersion blender to puree the chowder lightly, keeping some texture.
7. Top the chowder with the chopped chives before serving.

Thai-Inspired Coconut Soup

Time: 3 hours 15 minutes
Serving Size: 2 bowls
Prep Time: 15 minutes
Cook Time: 3 hours

Each Serving Has:
Calories: 320, Carbohydrates: 28g, Saturated Fat: 8g, Protein: 9g, Fat: 18g, Sodium: 400mg, Potassium: 620mg, Fiber: 6g, Sugar: 7g, Vitamin C: 16mg, Calcium: 60mg, Iron: 2.9mg

Ingredients:
- 1 cup [150g] cubed butternut squash
- 1/2 cup [80g] chopped red bell pepper
- 1/2 cup [80g] sliced mushrooms
- 1/4 cup [40g] chopped yellow onion
- 1 clove garlic, minced
- 1 tsp grated fresh ginger
- 1 tbsp red curry paste (plant-based)
- 1 cup [240ml] canned light coconut milk
- 1/2 cup [120ml] low-sodium vegetable broth
- 1 tbsp lime juice
- 1/4 tsp sea salt
- 1 tbsp chopped fresh cilantro

Directions:
1. Add the cubed butternut squash, chopped bell pepper, sliced mushrooms, chopped onion, and minced garlic to the slow cooker.
2. Stir in the grated ginger and red curry paste to distribute flavors evenly.
3. Pour in the coconut milk, vegetable broth, lime juice, and sprinkle with the sea salt.
4. Mix until all ingredients are well combined.
5. Cover and cook on low for 3 hours until vegetables are tender.
6. Stir the soup to blend the flavors evenly.
7. Garnish with the chopped fresh cilantro before serving.

Spicy Brown Rice & Mushroom Stew

| Time: 3 hours 15 minutes | Serving Size: 2 bowls |
| Prep Time: 15 minutes | Cook Time: 3 hours |

Each Serving Has:
Calories: 330, Carbohydrates: 42g, Saturated Fat: 1g, Protein: 10g, Fat: 12g, Sodium: 410mg, Potassium: 630mg, Fiber: 6g, Sugar: 5g, Vitamin C: 10mg, Calcium: 45mg, Iron: 3.2mg

Ingredients:
- 3/4 cup [120g] cooked brown rice
- 1 1/2 cups [135g] sliced cremini mushrooms
- 1/2 cup [75g] chopped red bell pepper
- 1/2 cup [80g] chopped zucchini
- 1/4 cup [40g] chopped yellow onion
- 1 clove garlic, minced
- 1 tbsp tomato paste (no salt added)
- 1 tbsp olive oil
- 1/2 tsp red pepper flakes
- 1/2 tsp ground cumin
- 1/4 tsp sea salt
- 1/4 tsp black pepper
- 1 cup [240ml] low-sodium vegetable broth
- 1 tbsp chopped fresh parsley

Directions:
1. Add the cooked rice, sliced mushrooms, chopped bell pepper, zucchini, onion, and minced garlic to the slow cooker.
2. Stir in the tomato paste, olive oil, red pepper flakes, cumin, sea salt, and black pepper.
3. Pour in the vegetable broth and mix until all ingredients are well combined.
4. Cover and cook on low for 3 hours, stirring once halfway through.
5. Stir again before serving to blend flavors and garnish with chopped fresh parsley.

Creamy Broccoli & Pea Soup

| Time: 3 hours 15 minutes | Serving Size: 2 bowls |
| Prep Time: 15 minutes | Cook Time: 3 hours |

Each Serving Has:
Calories: 280, Carbohydrates: 30g, Saturated Fat: 2g, Protein: 11g, Fat: 13g, Sodium: 320mg, Potassium: 650mg, Fiber: 8g, Sugar: 6g, Vitamin C: 52mg, Calcium: 90mg, Iron: 3.1mg

Ingredients:
- 1 1/2 cups [135g] chopped broccoli florets
- 3/4 cup [110g] green peas (fresh or frozen)
- 1/4 cup [40g] chopped leek (or yellow onion)
- 1 clove garlic, minced
- 1 tbsp olive oil
- 1 cup [240ml] low-sodium vegetable broth
- 1/2 cup [120ml] unsweetened plant-based milk
- 2 tbsp raw cashews, soaked and blended
- 1/2 tsp dried dill
- 1/4 tsp sea salt
- 1/4 tsp black pepper
- 1 tbsp chopped fresh parsley

Directions:
1. Add the chopped broccoli florets, leek, green peas, and minced garlic to the slow cooker.
2. Stir in the olive oil, vegetable broth, and plant-based milk.
3. Add blended cashews, dill, sea salt, and black pepper.
4. Mix well until all ingredients are combined.
5. Cover and cook on low for 3 hours until vegetables are soft.
6. Use an immersion blender to puree the soup until smooth and creamy.
7. Garnish with the chopped fresh parsley before serving.

Moroccan Chickpea Stew

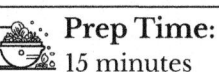

⏱ Time: 3 hours 15 minutes	🍽 Serving Size: 2 bowls
🥣 Prep Time: 15 minutes	🍲 Cook Time: 3 hours

Each Serving Has:
Calories: 340, Carbohydrates: 42g, Saturated Fat: 1g, Protein: 13g, Fat: 11g, Sodium: 390mg, Potassium: 720mg, Fiber: 10g, Sugar: 9g, Vitamin C: 18mg, Calcium: 90mg, Iron: 4.1mg

Ingredients:
- 1 1/4 cups [210g] cooked chickpeas
- 1/2 cup [75g] chopped carrots
- 1/2 cup [80g] chopped zucchini
- 1/4 cup [40g] chopped red bell pepper
- 1/4 cup [40g] chopped yellow onion
- 1 clove garlic, minced
- 1 tbsp olive oil
- 1 tbsp tomato paste (no salt added)
- 1 cup [240ml] low-sodium vegetable broth
- 1/2 tsp ground cumin
- 1/4 tsp ground cinnamon
- 1/4 tsp smoked paprika
- 1/4 tsp sea salt
- 1 tbsp chopped fresh cilantro

Directions:
1. Add the chickpeas, chopped carrots, zucchini, bell pepper, onion, and minced garlic to the slow cooker.
2. Stir in the olive oil and tomato paste until the vegetables are well coated.
3. Pour in the vegetable broth and mix thoroughly.
4. Add the cumin, cinnamon, smoked paprika, and sea salt.
5. Cover and cook on low for 3 hours until vegetables are soft.
6. Stir the stew to blend the flavors evenly.
7. Garnish with the chopped fresh cilantro before serving.

Butternut Squash Apple Soup

⏱ Time: 3 hours 15 minutes	🍽 Serving Size: 2 bowls
🥣 Prep Time: 15 minutes	🍲 Cook Time: 3 hours

Each Serving Has:
Calories: 300, Carbohydrates: 41g, Saturated Fat: 2g, Protein: 5g, Fat: 12g, Sodium: 300mg, Potassium: 690mg, Fiber: 7g, Sugar: 13g, Vitamin C: 30mg, Calcium: 80mg, Iron: 2.4mg

Ingredients:
- 1 1/2 cups [200g] cubed butternut squash
- 1 medium apple, peeled and chopped
- 1/4 cup [40g] chopped yellow onion
- 1 clove garlic, minced
- 1 tbsp olive oil
- 1/2 tsp ground ginger
- 1/4 tsp ground cinnamon
- 1/4 tsp sea salt
- 1 cup [240ml] low-sodium vegetable broth
- 1/2 cup [120ml] unsweetened almond milk
- 1 tbsp lemon juice
- 1 tbsp chopped fresh thyme

Directions:
1. Add the cubed butternut squash, chopped apple, onion, and minced garlic to the slow cooker.
2. Stir in the olive oil, ginger, cinnamon, and sea salt.
3. Pour in the vegetable broth and almond milk.
4. Mix well until all ingredients are well combined.
5. Cover and cook on low for 3 hours until squash is very tender.
6. Use an immersion blender to puree the soup until smooth.
7. Stir in the lemon juice and garnish with the chopped fresh thyme before serving.

CHAPTER 4: COZY BOWLS

Lemon Dill Split Pea Soup

Time: 3 hours 15 minutes
Serving Size: 2 bowls
Prep Time: 15 minutes
Cook Time: 3 hours

Each Serving Has:
Calories: 310, Carbohydrates: 42g, Saturated Fat: 0.5g, Protein: 18g, Fat: 7g, Sodium: 330mg, Potassium: 680mg, Fiber: 14g, Sugar: 4g, Vitamin C: 10mg, Calcium: 55mg, Iron: 3.6mg

Ingredients:
- 3/4 cup [150g] dried split peas, rinsed
- 1/2 cup [75g] chopped carrots
- 1/4 cup [40g] chopped celery
- 1/4 cup [40g] chopped yellow onion
- 1 clove garlic, minced
- 1 tbsp olive oil
- 1 1/2 cups [360ml] low-sodium vegetable broth
- 1 tbsp lemon juice
- 1/2 tsp dried dill
- 1/4 tsp sea salt
- 1/4 tsp black pepper
- 1 tbsp chopped fresh parsley

Directions:
1. Add the rinsed split peas, chopped carrots, celery, onion, and minced garlic to the slow cooker.
2. Stir in the olive oil, vegetable broth, lemon juice, dill, sea salt, and black pepper.
3. Mix thoroughly until all ingredients are well combined.
4. Cover and cook on low for 3 hours until the peas are tender.
5. Lightly mash the mixture with a spoon to create a creamy texture.
6. Stir to incorporate the flavors and consistency evenly.
7. Garnish with the chopped fresh parsley before serving.

Italian White Bean Stew

Time: 3 hours 15 minutes
Serving Size: 2 bowls
Prep Time: 15 minutes
Cook Time: 3 hours

Each Serving Has:
Calories: 330, Carbohydrates: 38g, Saturated Fat: 0.5g, Protein: 15g, Fat: 9g, Sodium: 360mg, Potassium: 720mg, Fiber: 11g, Sugar: 6g, Vitamin C: 14mg, Calcium: 90mg, Iron: 3.8mg

Ingredients:
- 1 1/4 cups [210g] cooked white beans (cannellini or great northern)
- 1/2 cup [75g] chopped carrots
- 1/2 cup [80g] chopped zucchini
- 1/4 cup [40g] chopped red bell pepper
- 1/4 cup [40g] chopped yellow onion
- 1 clove garlic, minced
- 1 tbsp olive oil
- 1 cup [240ml] low-sodium vegetable broth
- 1/2 tsp dried oregano
- 1/2 tsp dried basil
- 1/4 tsp sea salt
- 1/4 tsp black pepper
- 1 tbsp chopped fresh parsley

Directions:
1. Add the cooked white beans, chopped carrots, zucchini, bell pepper, onion, and minced garlic to the slow cooker.
2. Stir in the olive oil, vegetable broth, oregano, basil, sea salt, and black pepper.
3. Mix thoroughly until all ingredients are fully combined.
4. Cover and cook on low for 3 hours until vegetables are tender.
5. Stir gently to thicken the stew slightly.
6. Garnish with the chopped fresh parsley before serving.

Zucchini Basil Bisque

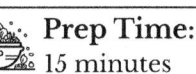

Time: 3 hours 15 minutes	Serving Size: 2 bowls
Prep Time: 15 minutes	Cook Time: 3 hours

Each Serving Has:

Calories: 260, Carbohydrates: 35g, Saturated Fat: 1g, Protein: 8g, Fat: 12g, Sodium: 320mg, Potassium: 680mg, Fiber: 8g, Sugar: 7g, Vitamin C: 24mg, Calcium: 80mg, Iron: 2.5mg

Ingredients:
- 2 medium zucchinis, chopped
- 1/2 cup [80g] chopped yellow onion
- 1 clove garlic, minced
- 1 tbsp olive oil
- 1/2 tsp dried basil
- 1/4 tsp sea salt
- 1/4 tsp black pepper
- 1 cup [240ml] low-sodium vegetable broth
- 1/2 cup [120ml] unsweetened almond milk
- 1 tbsp lemon juice
- 1 tbsp chopped fresh basil

Directions:
1. Add the chopped zucchini, onion, and minced garlic to the slow cooker.
2. Stir in the olive oil, basil, sea salt, and black pepper.
3. Pour in the vegetable broth and almond milk.
4. Mix thoroughly until all ingredients are evenly combined.
5. Cover and cook on low for 3 hours until the zucchini is tender.
6. Use an immersion blender to puree the soup until smooth.
7. Stir in the lemon juice and garnish with the chopped fresh basil before serving.

Curried Carrot Ginger Soup

Time: 3 hours 15 minutes	Serving Size: 2 bowls
Prep Time: 15 minutes	Cook Time: 3 hours

Each Serving Has:

Calories: 280, Carbohydrates: 40g, Saturated Fat: 1g, Protein: 6g, Fat: 10g, Sodium: 320mg, Potassium: 820mg, Fiber: 9g, Sugar: 12g, Vitamin C: 25mg, Calcium: 80mg, Iron: 3.0mg

Ingredients:
- 4 medium carrots, peeled and chopped
- 1/2 cup [80g] chopped onion
- 1 clove garlic, minced
- 1 tbsp grated fresh ginger
- 1 tbsp olive oil
- 1/2 tsp ground turmeric
- 1/2 tsp curry powder
- 1/4 tsp ground cumin
- 1/4 tsp sea salt
- 1/4 tsp black pepper
- 1 cup [240ml] low-sodium vegetable broth
- 1/2 cup [120ml] unsweetened coconut milk
- 1 tbsp lemon juice
- 1 tbsp chopped fresh cilantro

Directions:
1. Add the chopped carrots, onion, minced garlic, and grated ginger to the slow cooker.
2. Stir in the olive oil, turmeric, curry powder, cumin, sea salt, and black pepper.
3. Pour in the vegetable broth and coconut milk.
4. Mix thoroughly until all ingredients are well combined.
5. Cover and cook on low for 3 hours, until carrots are tender.
6. Use an immersion blender to puree the soup until smooth.
7. Stir in the lemon juice and garnish with the chopped fresh cilantro before serving.

CHAPTER 4: COZY BOWLS

Roasted Red Pepper Soup

⏰ Time: 3 hours 10 minutes	🍽 Serving Size: 2 bowls
🍲 Prep Time: 15 minutes	🍳 Cook Time: 2 hours 55 minutes

Each Serving Has:
Calories: 220, Carbohydrates: 34g, Saturated Fat: 1g, Protein: 4g, Fat: 8g, Sodium: 320mg, Potassium: 560mg, Fiber: 6g, Sugar: 12g, Vitamin C: 120mg, Calcium: 60mg, Iron: 2.5mg

Ingredients:
- 2 large red bell peppers, roasted and peeled
- 1/2 cup [80g] chopped yellow onion
- 1 clove garlic, minced
- 1 tbsp olive oil
- 1/2 tsp smoked paprika
- 1/4 tsp sea salt
- 1/4 tsp black pepper
- 1 cup [240ml] low-sodium vegetable broth
- 1/4 cup [60ml] unsweetened almond milk (plus extra for thinning, if needed)
- 1 tbsp chopped fresh basil

Directions:
1. Add the roasted bell peppers, chopped onion, and minced garlic to the slow cooker.
2. Stir in the olive oil, smoked paprika, sea salt, and black pepper.
3. Pour in the vegetable broth and almond milk, then mix well.
4. Cover and cook on low for 3 hours until vegetables are soft.
5. Use an immersion blender to puree the soup until smooth, adding more almond milk as needed to adjust the consistency.
6. Garnish with the chopped fresh basil before serving.

Kale & Potato Comfort Stew

⏰ Time: 3 hours 15 minutes	🍽 Serving Size: 2 bowls
🍲 Prep Time: 15 minutes	🍳 Cook Time: 3 hours

Each Serving Has:
Calories: 290, Carbohydrates: 50g, Saturated Fat: 1g, Protein: 7g, Fat: 8g, Sodium: 420mg, Potassium: 890mg, Fiber: 9g, Sugar: 6g, Vitamin C: 30mg, Calcium: 70mg, Iron: 3.2mg

Ingredients:
- 2 medium potatoes, peeled and diced
- 2 cups [150g] chopped kale (stems removed)
- 1/2 cup [75g] chopped carrots
- 1/4 cup [40g] chopped yellow onion
- 1 clove garlic, minced
- 1 tbsp olive oil
- 1 tsp dried thyme
- 1/2 tsp sea salt
- 1/4 tsp black pepper
- 1 cup [240ml] low-sodium vegetable broth
- 1/2 cup [120ml] unsweetened almond milk
- 1 tbsp lemon juice

Directions:
1. Add the diced potatoes, chopped kale, carrots, onion, and minced garlic to the slow cooker.
2. Stir in the olive oil, thyme, sea salt, and black pepper to coat the vegetables.
3. Pour in the vegetable broth and almond milk.
4. Mix thoroughly until all ingredients are well combined.
5. Cover and cook on low for 3 hours, until the potatoes are tender, stirring once halfway through cooking to blend the flavors.
6. Stir in the lemon juice before serving.

Cabbage and Fennel Soup

Time: 3 hours 15 minutes	Serving Size: 2 bowls
Prep Time: 15 minutes	Cook Time: 3 hours

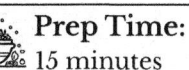

Each Serving Has:
Calories: 230, Carbohydrates: 48g, Saturated Fat: 0.5g, Protein: 5g, Fat: 6g, Sodium: 380mg, Potassium: 670mg, Fiber: 10g, Sugar: 12g, Vitamin C: 60mg, Calcium: 70mg, Iron: 2.3mg

Ingredients:
- 2 cups [200g] chopped cabbage
- 1 small fennel bulb, sliced
- 1/2 cup [75g] chopped carrots
- 1/2 cup [80g] chopped onion
- 1 clove garlic, minced
- 1 tbsp olive oil
- 1 tsp dried thyme
- 1/2 tsp sea salt
- 1/4 tsp black pepper
- 1 cup [240ml] low-sodium vegetable broth
- 1/2 cup [120ml] unsweetened almond milk
- 1 tbsp lemon juice

Directions:
1. Add the chopped cabbage, carrots, onion, sliced fennel, and minced garlic to the slow cooker.
2. Stir in the olive oil, thyme, sea salt, and black pepper.
3. Pour in the vegetable broth and almond milk.
4. Mix thoroughly until all ingredients are well combined.
5. Cover and cook on low for 3 hours until vegetables are tender.
6. After cooking, stir the soup to blend the flavors.
7. Stir in the lemon juice before serving.

Black Garlic Veggie Broth

Time: 3 hours	Serving Size: 2 bowls
Prep Time: 10 minutes	Cook Time: 2 hours 50 minutes

Each Serving Has:
Calories: 120, Carbohydrates: 26g, Saturated Fat: 0.5g, Protein: 3g, Fat: 1g, Sodium: 220mg, Potassium: 480mg, Fiber: 6g, Sugar: 8g, Vitamin C: 25mg, Calcium: 40mg, Iron: 1.5mg

Ingredients:
- 3 medium carrots, chopped
- 1/2 cup [80g] chopped celery
- 1/2 cup [80g] chopped onion
- 4 cloves black garlic, peeled (or 4 garlic cloves, minced + a few drops of balsamic vinegar)
- 1 tbsp olive oil
- 1 tsp dried thyme
- 1/4 tsp sea salt
- 1/4 tsp black pepper
- 1 1/2 cups [360ml] low-sodium vegetable broth
- 2 cups [480ml] water
- 1 tbsp lemon juice
- 1 tbsp chopped fresh parsley

Directions:
1. Add the chopped carrots, celery, onion, and peeled black garlic to the slow cooker.
2. Stir in the olive oil, thyme, sea salt, and black pepper.
3. Pour in the vegetable broth and water.
4. Mix thoroughly until all ingredients are well combined.
5. Cover and cook on low for 3 hours, allowing flavors to blend.
6. Use a slotted spoon to remove the black garlic, mash it, then return it to the soup.
7. Stir the soup well to incorporate the mashed garlic.
8. Stir in the lemon juice and garnish with the chopped fresh parsley before serving.

CHAPTER 4: COZY BOWLS

Chapter 5: Hearty Plates

Rustic Tofu Pot Roast

Time: 3 hours 30 minutes	Serving Size: 2 plates
Prep Time: 20 minutes	Cook Time: 3 hours 10 minutes

Each Serving Has:
Calories: 320, Carbohydrates: 38g, Saturated Fat: 2g, Protein: 22g, Fat: 16g, Sodium: 360mg, Potassium: 670mg, Fiber: 8g, Sugar: 7g, Vitamin C: 35mg, Calcium: 160mg, Iron: 3.4mg

Ingredients:
- 1 block [14 oz, 396g] firm tofu, drained and cubed
- 2 medium potatoes, peeled and chopped
- 1 cup [150g] chopped carrots
- 1/2 cup [80g] chopped onions
- 1 clove garlic, minced
- 1 tbsp olive oil
- 1 tsp dried rosemary
- 1/2 tsp ground thyme
- 1/4 tsp sea salt
- 1/4 tsp black pepper
- 1 1/2 cups [360ml] low-sodium vegetable broth
- 1 tbsp tamari (or low-sodium soy sauce)
- 1 tbsp chopped fresh parsley

Directions:
1. Heat the olive oil in a pan over medium heat, then sauté the tofu cubes until golden brown, about 5 minutes.
2. Transfer the tofu to the slow cooker and add chopped potatoes, carrots, onions, and minced garlic.
3. Stir in the rosemary, thyme, sea salt, and black pepper.
4. Pour the vegetable broth and tamari over the mixture.
5. Mix thoroughly until all ingredients are well combined.
6. Cover and cook on low for 3 hours, stirring once halfway through for even cooking, until the vegetables are tender.
7. Garnish with the chopped fresh parsley before serving.

Lentil & Root Veg Shepherd's Pie

Time: 3 hours 15 minutes	Serving Size: 2 plates
Prep Time: 15 minutes	Cook Time: 3 hours

Each Serving Has:
Calories: 350, Carbohydrates: 60g, Saturated Fat: 2g, Protein: 18g, Fat: 9g, Sodium: 450mg, Potassium: 950mg, Fiber: 12g, Sugar: 8g, Vitamin C: 35mg, Calcium: 80mg, Iron: 4.5mg

Ingredients:
- 1 cup [200g] green lentils, rinsed
- 2 medium carrots, peeled and diced
- 1 medium sweet potato, peeled and diced
- 1/2 cup [80g] diced onion
- 1 clove garlic, minced
- 1 tbsp olive oil
- 1 tsp dried thyme
- 1 tsp ground cumin
- 1/2 tsp sea salt
- 1/4 tsp black pepper
- 2 cups [480ml] low-sodium vegetable broth
- 1/2 cup [120ml] unsweetened almond milk
- 1 tbsp nutritional yeast
- 1 tbsp chopped fresh parsley

Directions:
1. Heat the olive oil in a pan over medium heat and sauté the diced onion and minced garlic until soft, about 5 minutes.
2. Add the diced carrots and sweet potato to the slow cooker, followed by the sautéed onion and garlic.
3. Stir in the green lentils, thyme, cumin, sea salt, and black pepper.
4. Pour in the vegetable broth and unsweetened almond milk.
5. Mix thoroughly until all ingredients are well combined.
6. Cover and cook on low for 3 hours, until the lentils and vegetables are tender.
7. Stir in the nutritional yeast.
8. Garnish with the chopped fresh parsley before serving.

Stuffed Squash with Wild Rice

Time: 3 hours 20 minutes	Serving Size: 2 servigs
Prep Time: 15 minutes	Cook Time: 3 hours 5 minutes

Each Serving Has:
Calories: 340, Carbohydrates: 74g, Saturated Fat: 1g, Protein: 10g, Fat: 6g, Sodium: 90mg, Potassium: 850mg, Fiber: 12g, Sugar: 10g, Vitamin C: 25mg, Calcium: 60mg, Iron: 2.5mg

Ingredients:
- 2 medium acorn squashes, halved and deseeded
- 1/2 cup [100g] wild rice, rinsed
- 1 small onion, diced
- 1 carrot, peeled and grated
- 1 celery stalk, chopped
- 1 tbsp olive oil
- 1/2 tsp ground cinnamon
- 1/2 tsp ground ginger
- 1/2 tsp ground turmeric
- 1/4 tsp black pepper
- 2 cups [480ml] low-sodium vegetable broth
- 1 tbsp tamari (or low-sodium soy sauce)
- 1 tbsp chopped fresh parsley

Directions:
1. Place the halved and deseeded acorn squash in the slow cooker.
2. Heat the olive oil in a pan over medium heat, then sauté the diced onion, grated carrot, and chopped celery until softened, about 5 minutes.
3. Stir in the cinnamon, ginger, turmeric, and black pepper, and cook for 1 minute.
4. Add the wild rice and vegetable broth to the pan and bring to a simmer.
5. Spoon the rice mixture into the hollowed centers of the squash halves.
6. Pour the tamari over the filled squashes.
7. Cover and cook on low for 3 hours, until the squash is tender and the rice is fully cooked.
8. Garnish with the chopped fresh parsley before serving.

CHAPTER 5: HEARTY PLATES

Tofu and Veggie Stroganoff

⏱ **Time:** 3 hours 25 minutes	🍴 **Serving Size:** 2 plates
🍲 **Prep Time:** 15 minutes	🍲 **Cook Time:** 3 hours 10 minutes

Each Serving Has:
Calories: 300, Carbohydrates: 45g, Saturated Fat: 2g, Protein: 18g, Fat: 10g, Sodium: 600mg, Potassium: 700mg, Fiber: 8g, Sugar: 6g, Vitamin C: 25mg, Calcium: 120mg, Iron: 3mg

Ingredients:
- 1 block [14 oz/397g] firm tofu, drained and crumbled
- 1 cup [150g] baby carrots, sliced
- 1 medium onion, chopped
- 2 cloves garlic, minced
- 1 cup [240ml] low-sodium vegetable broth
- 1/2 cup [120ml] unsweetened almond milk
- 1 tbsp olive oil
- 1 tbsp low-sodium soy sauce
- 1 tsp dried thyme
- 1 tsp smoked paprika
- 1/2 tsp black pepper
- 1 tbsp nutritional yeast
- 1/2 cup [50g] sliced mushrooms
- 1 tbsp chopped fresh parsley

Directions:
1. Heat the olive oil in a pan over medium heat, then sauté the chopped onion, minced garlic, and sliced carrots until soft, about 5 minutes.
2. Add the crumbled tofu to the pan and cook for another 2-3 minutes until slightly browned.
3. Stir in the soy sauce, smoked paprika, thyme, and black pepper.
4. Transfer the tofu mixture to the slow cooker and add the vegetable broth and almond milk.
5. Add the sliced mushrooms and nutritional yeast.
6. Mix thoroughly until all ingredients are well combined.
7. Cover and cook on low for 3 hours, until the vegetables are tender.
8. Garnish with the chopped fresh parsley before serving.

Mediterranean Chickpea Bake

⏱ **Time:** 3 hours 10 minutes	🍴 **Serving Size:** 2 servings
🍲 **Prep Time:** 10 minutes	🍲 **Cook Time:** 3 hours

Each Serving Has:
Calories: 300, Carbohydrates: 50g, Saturated Fat: 2g, Protein: 12g, Fat: 10g, Sodium: 600mg, Potassium: 700mg, Fiber: 9g, Sugar: 8g, Vitamin C: 15mg, Calcium: 90mg, Iron: 4mg

Ingredients:
- 1 can [15 oz/425g] chickpeas, drained and rinsed
- 1 medium zucchini, diced
- 1 medium red onion, chopped
- 1/2 cup [75g] cherry tomatoes, halved
- 1/4 cup [60ml] olive oil
- 1 tbsp dried oregano
- 1 tbsp lemon juice
- 1 tbsp tahini
- 1/2 tsp ground cumin
- 1/4 tsp black pepper
- 1/4 tsp salt
- 2 tbsp chopped fresh parsley
- 1/4 cup [25g] Kalamata olives, pitted and sliced

Directions:
1. Add the chickpeas, diced zucchini, chopped onion, and halved cherry tomatoes to a large bowl.
2. In a small bowl, whisk together the olive oil, lemon juice, tahini, oregano, cumin, black pepper, and salt.
3. Pour the dressing over the chickpea mixture and stir to coat all ingredients evenly.
4. Transfer the mixture to the slow cooker and spread it out evenly.
5. Cover and cook on low for 3 hours, until the vegetables are tender.
6. Once cooked, stir in the chopped fresh parsley.
7. Garnish with the sliced Kalamata olives before serving.

Mushroom Bourguignon

Time: 4 hours 15 minutes
Serving Size: 2 servings
Prep Time: 15 minutes
Cook Time: 4 hours

Each Serving Has:
Calories: 220, Carbohydrates: 30g, Saturated Fat: 3g, Protein: 6g, Fat: 12g, Sodium: 500mg, Potassium: 720mg, Fiber: 6g, Sugar: 7g, Vitamin C: 8mg, Calcium: 50mg, Iron: 3mg

Ingredients:
- 1 lb [450g] Portobello mushrooms, sliced
- 1 medium onion, chopped
- 2 cloves garlic, minced
- 1 cup [240ml] low-sodium vegetable broth
- 1 tbsp tomato paste (no salt added)
- 1 tbsp chopped fresh thyme leaves (or 1 tsp dried)
- 1 tbsp low-sodium soy sauce (or tamari)
- 2 tbsp olive oil
- 1/4 tsp black pepper
- 1/2 tsp salt
- 1 tbsp cornstarch (optional for thickening)
- 2 tbsp chopped fresh parsley

Directions:
1. Heat the olive oil in a skillet over medium heat, then sauté the chopped onion and minced garlic until soft, about 3–4 minutes.
2. Add the sliced mushrooms and cook until they release moisture and become browned, about 7–8 minutes.
3. Transfer the mushroom mixture to the slow cooker.
4. Add the vegetable broth, tomato paste, thyme, soy sauce, salt, and black pepper.
5. Mix thoroughly until all ingredients are well combined.
6. Cover and cook on low for 3–4 hours, until the mushrooms are tender.
7. If desired, stir in a cornstarch slurry for thickening and cook for another 10 minutes.
8. Garnish with the chopped fresh parsley before serving.

Slow-Cooked Eggplant Parmesan

Time: 5 hours 15 minutes
Serving Size: 2 servings
Prep Time: 15 minutes
Cook Time: 5 hours

Each Serving Has:
Calories: 280, Carbohydrates: 35g, Saturated Fat: 4g, Protein: 10g, Fat: 14g, Sodium: 670mg, Potassium: 750mg, Fiber: 8g, Sugar: 12g, Vitamin C: 10mg, Calcium: 160mg, Iron: 3mg

Ingredients:
- 1 medium eggplant, sliced into 1/4-inch thick rounds
- 1 cup [240ml] low-sodium marinara sauce
- 1/2 cup [60g] whole wheat breadcrumbs
- 1/4 cup [25g] nutritional yeast
- 1/4 cup [60ml] unsweetened almond milk
- 1 tbsp [15ml] olive oil
- 1 tsp dried oregano
- 1 tsp dried basil
- 1/4 tsp garlic powder
- 1/4 tsp black pepper
- 1/4 tsp salt
- 1/4 cup [30g] shredded vegan mozzarella (optional)

Directions:
1. Preheat a skillet over medium heat and add the olive oil.
2. In a bowl, mix the breadcrumbs, nutritional yeast, oregano, basil, garlic powder, black pepper, and salt.
3. DipEach eggplant slice into the almond milk, then coat with the seasoned breadcrumb mixture.
4. Brown the breaded eggplant slices in the skillet for 3–4 minutes onEach side, until golden.
5. Transfer the browned eggplant slices to the slow cooker.
6. Pour the marinara sauce evenly over the eggplant slices.
7. Cover and cook on low for 4–5 hours until the eggplant is tender.
8. Sprinkle shredded mozzarella over the top during the final 10 minutes of cooking, if desired.

CHAPTER 5: HEARTY PLATES

Creamy Polenta with Ratatouille

⏰ **Time:** 3 hours 40 minutes	🍽 **Serving Size:** 2 plates
🍲 **Prep Time:** 10 minutes	🍳 **Cook Time:** 3 hours 30 minutes

Each Serving Has:
Calories: 310, Carbohydrates: 45g, Saturated Fat: 3g, Protein: 7g, Fat: 11g, Sodium: 500mg, Potassium: 820mg, Fiber: 7g, Sugar: 8g, Vitamin C: 50mg, Calcium: 120mg, Iron: 3mg

Ingredients:
- 1/2 cup [120g] polenta
- 2 cups [480ml] low-sodium vegetable broth
- 1 tbsp [15ml] olive oil (plus extra for greasing)
- 1 medium zucchini, sliced
- 1 medium eggplant, cubed
- 1 bell pepper, chopped
- 1/2 cup [120g] canned low-sodium diced tomatoes, drained
- 1/2 tsp dried thyme
- 1/2 tsp dried oregano
- 1/4 tsp garlic powder
- 1/4 tsp salt
- 1/4 tsp black pepper
- 1 tbsp nutritional yeast (optional)

Directions:
1. Lightly grease the slow cooker insert with a small amount of olive oil.
2. Add the sliced zucchini, cubed eggplant, chopped bell pepper, and diced tomatoes to the slow cooker.
3. Sprinkle in the thyme, oregano, garlic powder, salt, and black pepper. Stir to combine.
4. In a separate bowl, whisk polenta into the vegetable broth until well blended.
5. Pour the polenta mixture evenly over the vegetables in the slow cooker—do not stir.
6. Drizzle olive oil over the top, cover, and cook on low for 3 hours and 30 minutes, or until the polenta is creamy and the vegetables are tender.
7. Gently stir everything together, then mix in nutritional yeast (if using) before serving.

Sweet Potato and Peanut Casserole

⏰ **Time:** 3 hours 10 minutes	🍽 **Serving Size:** 2 servings
🍲 **Prep Time:** 10 minutes	🍳 **Cook Time:** 3 hours

Each Serving Has:
Calories: 380, Carbohydrates: 48g, Saturated Fat: 6g, Protein: 10g, Fat: 16g, Sodium: 400mg, Potassium: 900mg, Fiber: 7g, Sugar: 10g, Vitamin C: 30mg, Calcium: 80mg, Iron: 3mg

Ingredients:
- 2 medium sweet potatoes, peeled and diced
- 1/2 cup [120g] unsweetened peanut butter
- 1/2 cup [120ml] low-sodium vegetable broth
- 1/4 cup [60ml] coconut milk (or any plant-based milk)
- 1 tbsp maple syrup
- 1 tsp ground ginger
- 1/4 tsp ground cinnamon
- 1/4 tsp salt
- 1/4 tsp black pepper
- 1 tsp roasted peanuts, chopped

Directions:
1. Add the diced sweet potatoes to the slow cooker.
2. In a bowl, whisk together the peanut butter, vegetable broth, coconut milk, and maple syrup.
3. Stir in the ginger, cinnamon, salt, and black pepper.
4. Pour the peanut butter mixture over the sweet potatoes.
5. Mix thoroughly until all ingredients are well combined.
6. Cover and cook on low for 3 hours, or until the sweet potatoes are tender when pierced with a fork.
7. Top with the chopped roasted peanuts before serving.

Balsamic Glazed Cauliflower Steaks

⏲ Time: 3 hours 10 minutes	🍴 Serving Size: 2 servings
🥣 Prep Time: 10 minutes	🍲 Cook Time: 3 hours

Each Serving Has:
Calories: 220, Carbohydrates: 18g, Saturated Fat: 3g, Protein: 5g, Fat: 16g, Sodium: 320mg, Potassium: 400mg, Fiber: 6g, Sugar: 8g, Vitamin C: 55mg, Calcium: 80mg, Iron: 2mg

Ingredients:
- 1 medium cauliflower, cut into 2 steaks
- 1 tbsp olive oil
- 2 tbsp balsamic vinegar
- 1 tbsp maple syrup
- 1 tsp dried thyme
- 1/2 tsp garlic powder
- 1/4 tsp salt
- 1/4 tsp black pepper
- 1 tbsp chopped fresh parsley

Directions:
1. Brush both sides of the cauliflower steaks with olive oil.
2. In a small bowl, whisk together the balsamic vinegar, maple syrup, thyme, garlic powder, salt, and pepper.
3. Place the cauliflower steaks in the slow cooker in a single layer.
4. Pour the balsamic glaze over the steaks, lifting slightly to coat underneath.
5. Cover and cook on low for 2 hours and 30 minutes to 3 hours, until fork-tender.
6. Garnish with the chopped fresh parsley before serving.

Tamari Tempeh & Veggie Skillet

⏲ Time: 3 hours 10 minutes	🍴 Serving Size: 2 plates
🥣 Prep Time: 10 minutes	🍲 Cook Time: 3 hours

Each Serving Has:
Calories: 290, Carbohydrates: 25g, Saturated Fat: 2g, Protein: 22g, Fat: 16g, Sodium: 560mg, Potassium: 470mg, Fiber: 7g, Sugar: 5g, Vitamin C: 45mg, Calcium: 100mg, Iron: 3mg

Ingredients:
- 1 package tempeh (8 oz) [227g], cut into cubes
- 1 tbsp olive oil (plus extra for greasing)
- 2 tbsp tamari sauce
- 1 cup bell peppers, sliced
- 1 cup zucchini, sliced
- 1/2 cup red onion, sliced
- 1 clove garlic, minced
- 1 tsp smoked paprika
- 1/2 tsp ground cumin
- 1/4 tsp salt
- 1/4 tsp black pepper
- 1 tsp toasted sesame seeds

Directions:
1. Lightly grease the slow cooker insert with olive oil.
2. In a large bowl, mix tempeh cubes with olive oil, tamari, smoked paprika, and cumin. Toss to coat well.
3. Add the seasoned tempeh to the slow cooker.
4. Layer the sliced bell peppers, zucchini, red onion, and minced garlic on top.
5. Sprinkle with salt and black pepper.
6. Mix thoroughly until all ingredients are well combined.
7. Cover and cook on low for 3 hours, until the vegetables are tender and the tempeh has absorbed the flavors.
8. Gently stir and sprinkle with the sesame seeds before serving.

Portobello and Barley Bake

⏱ Time: 3 hours 10 minutes	🍴 Serving Size: 2 plates
🥣 Prep Time: 10 minutes	🍲 Cook Time: 3 hours

Each Serving Has:
Calories: 280, Carbohydrates: 45g, Saturated Fat: 2g, Protein: 9g, Fat: 8g, Sodium: 300mg, Potassium: 650mg, Fiber: 8g, Sugar: 7g, Vitamin C: 8mg, Calcium: 80mg, Iron: 3mg

Ingredients:
- 2 large Portobello mushrooms, stems removed and caps sliced
- 1/2 cup [100g] pearl barley, rinsed
- 1 tbsp olive oil
- 1/4 cup [40g] diced red onion
- 1 clove garlic, minced
- 1 cup [240 ml] low-sodium vegetable broth
- 1/2 tsp dried thyme
- 1/2 tsp dried rosemary
- 1/4 tsp salt
- 1/4 tsp black pepper
- 1/4 cup chopped fresh parsley

Directions:
1. Heat the olive oil in a skillet over medium heat and add the chopped onion and minced garlic. Sauté for 3–4 minutes until softened.
2. Add the sliced Portobello mushrooms and cook for another 3–4 minutes, until slightly tender.
3. Transfer the mushroom mixture to the slow cooker.
4. Add the rinsed pearl barley, vegetable broth, thyme, rosemary, salt, and black pepper.
5. Mix thoroughly until all ingredients are well combined.
6. Cover and cook on low for 3 hours, until the barley is tender and most of the liquid is absorbed.
7. Stir in the chopped fresh parsley before serving.

Vegan Jambalaya

⏱ Time: 4 hours 10 minutes	🍴 Serving Size: 2 bowls
🥣 Prep Time: 10 minutes	🍲 Cook Time: 4 hours

Each Serving Has:
Calories: 350, Carbohydrates: 60g, Saturated Fat: 3g, Protein: 10g, Fat: 9g, Sodium: 550mg, Potassium: 800mg, Fiber: 8g, Sugar: 8g, Vitamin C: 20mg, Calcium: 60mg, Iron: 3mg

Ingredients:
- 1/2 cup [100g] long-grain brown rice, rinsed
- 1/2 cup [75g] diced bell pepper
- 1/2 cup [80g] diced onion
- 1/2 cup [50g] diced celery
- 1 clove garlic, minced
- 1 can (14 oz [400g]) diced tomatoes
- 1 cup [240ml] low-sodium vegetable broth
- 1 tbsp olive oil
- 1/2 tsp thyme
- 1/4 tsp cayenne pepper
- 1/2 tsp salt
- 1/4 tsp black pepper
- 1 cup [60g] chopped kale, stems removed
- 1/4 cup chopped fresh parsley

Directions:
1. Heat the olive oil in a skillet over medium heat. Sauté the chopped onion, bell pepper, and celery for 5 minutes, until slightly softened.
2. Add the minced garlic, thyme, cayenne pepper, salt, and black pepper. Stir and cook for another minute.
3. Transfer the sautéed vegetable mixture to the slow cooker.
4. Add the rinsed rice, diced tomatoes with their liquid, vegetable broth, and chopped kale.
5. Mix thoroughly until all ingredients are well combined.
6. Cover and cook on low for 4 hours, until the rice is tender and the mixture is thickened.
7. Stir gently and garnish with the chopped fresh parsley before serving.

Cheesy Vegan Cauliflower Gratin

⏱ Time: 3 hours 10 minutes	🍽 Serving Size: 2 servings
🥣 Prep Time: 10 minutes	🍲 Cook Time: 3 hours

Each Serving Has:
Calories: 290, Carbohydrates: 20g, Saturated Fat: 2g, Protein: 7g, Fat: 20g, Sodium: 350mg, Potassium: 700mg, Fiber: 6g, Sugar: 4g, Vitamin C: 75mg, Calcium: 150mg, Iron: 2mg

Ingredients:
- 1 small head of cauliflower [500g], cut into florets
- 1/2 cup [120ml] unsweetened almond milk
- 1/4 cup [20g] nutritional yeast
- 1 tbsp olive oil
- 1 tbsp flour
- 1/2 tsp garlic powder
- 1/4 tsp ground turmeric
- 1/4 tsp smoked paprika
- 1/2 tsp salt
- 1/4 tsp black pepper
- 1/2 cup [30g] breadcrumbs
- 1 tbsp chopped fresh parsley

Directions:
1. In a saucepan over medium heat, warm the olive oil. Add the flour, garlic powder, turmeric, smoked paprika, salt, and black pepper. Stir constantly for 1 minute to form a roux.
2. Slowly whisk in the almond milk and cook for 3–5 minutes, whisking, until the sauce thickens.
3. Remove from the heat and stir in the nutritional yeast until smooth.
4. Add the cauliflower florets to the slow cooker.
5. Pour the sauce evenly over the cauliflower and gently stir to coat.
6. Sprinkle the breadcrumbs on top.
7. Cover and cook on low for 3 hours, until the cauliflower is fork-tender.
8. Garnish with the chopped fresh parsley before serving.

Slow Cooker Stuffed Cabbage Rolls

⏱ Time: 1 hour 25 minutes	🍽 Serving Size: 2 servings
🥣 Prep Time: 20 minutes	🍲 Cook Time: 1 hour 5 minutes

Each Serving Has:
Calories: 290, Carbohydrates: 52g, Saturated Fat: 2g, Protein: 10g, Fat: 7g, Sodium: 550mg, Potassium: 680mg, Fiber: 8g, Sugar: 10g, Vitamin C: 60mg, Calcium: 100mg, Iron: 4mg

Ingredients:
- 4 large cabbage leaves, trimmed
- 1/2 cup [85g] cooked quinoa
- 1/2 cup [85g] cooked lentils
- 1/4 cup [40g] diced onions
- 1/4 cup [40g] diced carrots
- 1/2 cup [120ml] low-sodium tomato sauce
- 1 tbsp olive oil
- 1/2 tsp garlic powder
- 1/4 tsp smoked paprika
- 1/2 tsp dried oregano
- 1/4 tsp salt
- 1/4 tsp black pepper

Directions:
1. In a mixing bowl, combine the cooked quinoa, cooked lentils, diced onions, carrots, garlic powder, smoked paprika, oregano, salt, and black pepper.
2. Lay the cabbage leaves flat and place a heaping spoonful of the filling in the center ofEach leaf. Roll tightly and tuck in the edges.
3. Place the cabbage rolls seam-side down in the slow cooker.
4. In a separate bowl, mix the tomato sauce with olive oil.
5. Pour the sauce mixture over the cabbage rolls.
6. Cover and cook on low for 1 hour and 5 minutes, until the cabbage is tender.
7. Drizzle with the sauce from the slow cooker before serving.

CHAPTER 5: HEARTY PLATES

Chapter 6: Flavorful Sides

Lemon Herb Quinoa Pilaf

Time: 2 hours 10 minutes	Serving Size: 2 bowls
Prep Time: 10 minutes	Cook Time: 2 hours

Each Serving Has:
Calories: 230, Carbohydrates: 45g, Saturated Fat: 1g, Protein: 6g, Fat: 4g, Sodium: 15mg, Potassium: 200mg, Fiber: 5g, Sugar: 3g, Vitamin C: 6mg, Calcium: 50mg, Iron: 2mg

Ingredients:
- 1/2 cup [85g] quinoa, rinsed
- 1 cup [240ml] low-sodium vegetable broth
- 1 tbsp olive oil
- 1/2 lemon, juiced
- 1 tsp lemon zest
- 1/2 tsp dried oregano
- 1/2 tsp garlic powder
- 1/4 tsp salt
- 1/4 tsp black pepper
- 1 tbsp chopped fresh parsley

Directions:
1. Lightly grease the slow cooker insert.
2. Add the rinsed quinoa and vegetable broth to the slow cooker. Stir to combine.
3. Cover and cook on low for 2 hours, or until the quinoa is tender and the liquid is absorbed.
4. Fluff the quinoa with a fork. Stir in the olive oil, lemon juice, lemon zest, oregano, garlic powder, salt, and black pepper.
5. Cover and cook on low for 10 more minutes to allow the flavors to blend.
6. Garnish with the chopped fresh parsley before serving.

Garlic Roasted Cauliflower Rice

⏰ Time: 2 hours 10 minutes	🍴 Serving Size: 2 plates
🍚 Prep Time: 10 minutes	🍲 Cook Time: 2 hours

Each Serving Has:

Calories: 100, Carbohydrates: 14g, Saturated Fat: 1g, Protein: 3g, Fat: 5g, Sodium: 150mg, Potassium: 350mg, Fiber: 4g, Sugar: 3g, Vitamin C: 70mg, Calcium: 40mg, Iron: 1mg

Ingredients:
- 1 medium cauliflower [350g], cut into florets
- 1 tbsp olive oil (plus extra for greasing)
- 2 cloves garlic, minced
- 1/4 tsp salt
- 1/4 tsp black pepper
- 1 tbsp lemon juice
- 1 tbsp chopped fresh parsley

Directions:
1. In a food processor, pulse the cauliflower florets until they resemble rice-sized grains.
2. Transfer the cauliflower rice to a bowl and toss with olive oil, minced garlic, salt, and black pepper.
3. Lightly grease the slow cooker insert. Add the cauliflower mixture and spread it out evenly.
4. Cover and cook on low for 2 hours, stirring once halfway through, until the cauliflower is tender and lightly golden at the edges.
5. Stir in the lemon juice and garnish with the chopped fresh parsley before serving.

Sweet & Spicy Glazed Carrots

⏰ Time: 2 hours 10 minutes	🍴 Serving Size: 2 bowls
🍚 Prep Time: 10 minutes	🍲 Cook Time: 2 hours

Each Serving Has:

Calories: 130, Carbohydrates: 30g, Saturated Fat: 0g, Protein: 2g, Fat: 2g, Sodium: 160mg, Potassium: 450mg, Fiber: 5g, Sugar: 12g, Vitamin C: 10mg, Calcium: 40mg, Iron: 1mg

Ingredients:
- 2 medium carrots [180g], peeled and cut into rounds
- 1 tbsp olive oil (plus extra for greasing)
- 1 tbsp maple syrup
- 1/2 tsp chili powder
- 1/4 tsp smoked paprika
- 1/4 tsp salt
- 1/4 tsp black pepper
- 1 tsp apple cider vinegar

Directions:
1. In a bowl, toss the carrot rounds with olive oil, maple syrup, chili powder, smoked paprika, salt, and black pepper.
2. Lightly grease the slow cooker insert and add the carrot mixture.
3. Cover and cook on low for 2 hours, or until the carrots are tender and glazed, stirring once halfway through.
4. Drizzle with apple cider vinegar and toss to combine before serving.

CHAPTER 6: FLAVORFUL SIDES

Creamy Mashed Parsnips

Time: 4 hours 10 minutes		**Serving Size:** 2 bowls	
Prep Time: 10 minutes		**Cook Time:** 4 hours	

Each Serving Has:
Calories: 180, Carbohydrates: 38g, Saturated Fat: 0g, Protein: 3g, Fat: 1g, Sodium: 50mg, Potassium: 400mg, Fiber: 7g, Sugar: 7g, Vitamin C: 20mg, Calcium: 40mg, Iron: 1mg

Ingredients:
- 2 medium parsnips [300g], peeled and chopped
- 1 tbsp olive oil
- 1/2 cup [120g] low-sodium vegetable broth
- 1/4 tsp salt
- 1/4 tsp black pepper
- 1/4 tsp garlic powder

Directions:
1. Add the chopped parsnips, vegetable broth, salt, black pepper, and garlic powder to the slow cooker.
2. Cover and cook on low for 4 hours, or until the parsnips are very soft.
3. Drain any excess liquid if needed, then mash the parsnips directly in the slow cooker using a masher or immersion blender.
4. Stir in the olive oil and mix until smooth before serving.

Savory Green Bean Almondine

Time: 2 hours 10 minutes		**Serving Size:** 2 plates	
Prep Time: 10 minutes		**Cook Time:** 2 hours	

Each Serving Has:
Calories: 160, Carbohydrates: 14g, Saturated Fat: 1g, Protein: 4g, Fat: 12g, Sodium: 80mg, Potassium: 400mg, Fiber: 5g, Sugar: 4g, Vitamin C: 25mg, Calcium: 70mg, Iron: 1mg

Ingredients:
- 2 cups [300g] green beans, trimmed
- 1/4 cup [35g] sliced almonds
- 1 tbsp olive oil
- 1 tbsp lemon juice
- 1/4 tsp garlic powder
- 1/4 tsp salt
- 1/4 tsp black pepper
- 2 tbsp filtered water

Directions:
1. Place the green beans in the slow cooker and add the water.
2. In a small bowl, mix the olive oil, garlic powder, salt, and black pepper. Drizzle over the green beans and toss gently to coat.
3. Sprinkle the sliced almonds evenly over the top.
4. Cover and cook on low for 2 hours, or until the green beans are tender.
5. Drizzle with lemon juice just before serving.

Apple Cider Brussels Sprouts

Time: 3 hours 10 minutes
Serving Size: 2 bowls
Prep Time: 10 minutes
Cook Time: 3 hours

Each Serving Has:
Calories: 120, Carbohydrates: 18g, Saturated Fat: 1g, Protein: 5g, Fat: 7g, Sodium: 35mg, Potassium: 350mg, Fiber: 6g, Sugar: 7g, Vitamin C: 85mg, Calcium: 50mg, Iron: 2mg

Ingredients:
- 2 cups [200g] Brussels sprouts, trimmed and halved
- 1 tbsp apple cider vinegar
- 1 tbsp olive oil (plus extra for greasing)
- 1 tbsp maple syrup
- 1/4 tsp garlic powder
- 1/4 tsp salt
- 1/4 tsp black pepper
- 1 tsp lime zest

Directions:
1. Lightly grease the slow cooker insert with olive oil.
2. Place the Brussels sprouts inside.
3. In a small bowl, whisk together the apple cider vinegar, olive oil, maple syrup, garlic powder, salt, and black pepper.
4. Pour the mixture over the Brussels sprouts and stir well to coat.
5. Cover and cook on low for 3 hours, stirring once halfway through, until the Brussels sprouts are tender and flavorful.
6. Garnish with the lime zest before serving.

Spiced Basmati Rice Medley

Time: 2 hours 10 minutes
Serving Size: 2 bowls
Prep Time: 10 minutes
Cook Time: 2 hours

Each Serving Has:
Calories: 220, Carbohydrates: 45g, Saturated Fat: 1g, Protein: 5g, Fat: 3g, Sodium: 15mg, Potassium: 200mg, Fiber: 3g, Sugar: 2g, Vitamin C: 2mg, Calcium: 20mg, Iron: 2mg

Ingredients:
- 1 cup [170g] basmati rice, rinsed
- 2 cups [480ml] low-sodium vegetable broth
- 1 tbsp olive oil (plus extra for greasing)
- 1/2 tsp ground turmeric
- 1/2 tsp ground cumin
- 1/2 tsp ground cinnamon
- 1/4 tsp ground coriander
- 1/4 tsp black pepper
- 1/4 cup [25g] slivered almonds
- 1/4 cup [40g] raisins (optional)

Directions:
1. Lightly grease the slow cooker insert with olive oil.
2. Add the rinsed basmati rice and vegetable broth.
3. Stir in the olive oil, turmeric, cumin, cinnamon, coriander, and black pepper.
4. Cover and cook on low for 2 hours, or until the rice is tender and fluffy.
5. Add the slivered almonds and raisins (if using). Stir gently to combine.
6. Cover and let sit on warm for 5–10 minutes to soften the raisins slightly and warm the nuts.

CHAPTER 6: FLAVORFUL SIDES

Ginger Sesame Bok Choy

⏰ Time: 1 hour 5 minutes	🍴 Serving Size: 2 plates
🍚 Prep Time: 5 minutes	🍲 Cook Time: 1 hour

Each Serving Has:
Calories: 130, Carbohydrates: 13g, Saturated Fat: 1g, Protein: 4g, Fat: 8g, Sodium: 300mg, Potassium: 400mg, Fiber: 3g, Sugar: 6g, Vitamin C: 40mg, Calcium: 120mg, Iron: 2mg

Ingredients:
- 4 cups [240g] bok choy, chopped
- 1 tbsp sesame oil
- 1 tbsp grated fresh ginger
- 1/2 tsp garlic, minced
- 1 tbsp low-sodium soy sauce
- 1 tsp rice vinegar
- 1 tsp sesame seeds
- 1 tsp olive oil

Directions:
1. Lightly grease the slow cooker insert with olive oil.
2. In a small bowl, whisk together the sesame oil, grated ginger, minced garlic, soy sauce, and rice vinegar.
3. Place the chopped bok choy in the slow cooker and pour the sauce over the top. Toss gently to coat.
4. Cover and cook on low for 1 hour, until the bok choy is wilted and tender but not mushy.
5. Sprinkle with the sesame seeds before serving.

Herbed Sweet Potato Mash

⏰ Time: 4 hours 10 minutes	🍴 Serving Size: 2 bowls
🍚 Prep Time: 10 minutes	🍲 Cook Time: 4 hours

Each Serving Has:
Calories: 180, Carbohydrates: 38g, Saturated Fat: 1g, Protein: 3g, Fat: 4g, Sodium: 180mg, Potassium: 800mg, Fiber: 6g, Sugar: 9g, Vitamin C: 45mg, Calcium: 60mg, Iron: 1mg

Ingredients:
- 2 medium sweet potatoes [400g], peeled and cubed
- 1/4 cup [60ml] low-sodium vegetable broth
- 1 tbsp olive oil
- 1 tbsp fresh thyme, chopped
- 1 tbsp fresh rosemary, chopped
- 1/4 tsp salt
- 1/4 tsp black pepper
- 1 tbsp chopped green onions

Directions:
1. Add the cubed sweet potatoes to the slow cooker.
2. Drizzle with olive oil and sprinkle in thyme, rosemary, salt, and black pepper.
3. Pour in the vegetable broth and stir to coat evenly.
4. Cover and cook on low for 4 hours, until the sweet potatoes are very tender.
5. Drain any excess liquid if needed, then mash the sweet potatoes directly in the slow cooker to the desired consistency.
6. Garnish with the chopped green onions before serving.

Caramelized Onion and Kale

Time: 3 hours 10 minutes
Serving Size: 2 bowls
Prep Time: 10 minutes
Cook Time: 3 hours

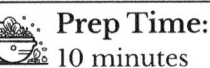

Each Serving Has:
Calories: 150, Carbohydrates: 18g, Saturated Fat: 1g, Protein: 4g, Fat: 8g, Sodium: 300mg, Potassium: 400mg, Fiber: 5g, Sugar: 7g, Vitamin C: 60mg, Calcium: 100mg, Iron: 2mg

Ingredients:
- 1 tbsp olive oil
- 1 medium onion, thinly sliced
- 2 cups [60g] kale, chopped
- 1/2 cup [120ml] low-sodium vegetable broth
- 1/4 tsp salt
- 1/4 tsp black pepper
- 1/4 tsp garlic powder

Directions:
1. Add the olive oil, sliced onion, salt, and garlic powder to the slow cooker. Stir to coat.
2. Cover and cook on low for 2 hours, stirring once halfway through, until the onions are soft and beginning to caramelize.
3. Add the chopped kale and vegetable broth. Stir to combine.
4. Cover again and cook on low for 1 hour, until the kale is tender and infused with flavor.
5. Stir in the black pepper before serving.

Maple Glazed Acorn Squash

Time: 3 hours 15 minutes
Serving Size: 2 servings
Prep Time: 15 minutes
Cook Time: 3 hours

Each Serving Has:
Calories: 180, Carbohydrates: 45g, Saturated Fat: 1g, Protein: 2g, Fat: 3g, Sodium: 150mg, Potassium: 600mg, Fiber: 8g, Sugar: 22g, Vitamin C: 30mg, Calcium: 50mg, Iron: 1mg

Ingredients:
- 1 medium acorn squash, halved and seeds removed
- 1 tbsp maple syrup
- 1 tbsp olive oil (plus extra for greasing)
- 1/4 tsp ground cinnamon
- 1/4 tsp ground nutmeg
- 1/4 tsp salt

Directions:
1. Lightly grease the bottom of the slow cooker insert with olive oil.
2. In a small bowl, mix the maple syrup, olive oil, cinnamon, nutmeg, and salt.
3. Brush the cut sides of the acorn squash halves with the mixture.
4. Place the squash halves, cut side up, in the slow cooker.
5. Cover and cook on low for 3 hours, or until the squash is fork-tender.
6. Spoon any extra glaze from the bottom of the cooker over the squash before serving.

CHAPTER 6: FLAVORFUL SIDES

Wild Mushroom Rice Blend

Time: 3 hours 10 minutes
Serving Size: 2 bowls
Prep Time: 10 minutes
Cook Time: 3 hours

Each Serving Has:
Calories: 220, Carbohydrates: 45g, Saturated Fat: 1g, Protein: 6g, Fat: 3g, Sodium: 400mg, Potassium: 370mg, Fiber: 4g, Sugar: 2g, Vitamin C: 3mg, Calcium: 30mg, Iron: 2mg

Ingredients:
- 1/2 cup [85g] wild rice, rinsed
- 1/2 cup [85g] white rice, rinsed
- 1 cup [240ml] low-sodium vegetable broth
- 1/2 cup [75g] wild mushrooms, chopped
- 1/2 cup [75g] cremini mushrooms, chopped
- 1 tbsp olive oil
- 1/4 tsp salt
- 1/4 tsp black pepper
- 1/2 tsp dried thyme
- 1 tbsp chopped fresh parsley

Directions:
1. In a skillet, heat the olive oil over medium heat. Add the wild and cremini mushrooms and sauté for 3–4 minutes, until softened.
2. Transfer the mushrooms to the slow cooker.
3. Add the rinsed wild rice, white rice, vegetable broth, salt, black pepper, and thyme. Stir gently to combine.
4. Cover and cook on low for 3 hours, or until both types of rice are tender and the liquid is absorbed.
5. Fluff with a fork and stir in the chopped fresh parsley before serving.

Rosemary Garlic Fingerlings

Time: 3 hours 10 minutes
Serving Size: 2 servings
Prep Time: 10 minutes
Cook Time: 3 hours

Each Serving Has:
Calories: 215, Carbohydrates: 42g, Saturated Fat: 0.5g, Protein: 4g, Fat: 6g, Sodium: 95mg, Potassium: 850mg, Fiber: 5g, Sugar: 2g, Vitamin C: 18mg, Calcium: 30mg, Iron: 1.6mg

Ingredients:
- 10 oz [283g] fingerling potatoes, halved
- 1 tbsp extra-virgin olive oil
- 2 cloves garlic, minced
- 1 tbsp fresh rosemary, finely chopped
- 1/4 cup [60ml] low-sodium vegetable broth
- 1/4 tsp sea salt
- 1/4 tsp black pepper

Directions:
1. Add the halved fingerling potatoes to the slow cooker.
2. Drizzle the olive oil evenly over the potatoes.
3. Sprinkle in the minced garlic and chopped fresh rosemary.
4. Pour in the vegetable broth and season with sea salt and black pepper.
5. Stir gently to combine.
6. Cover and cook on low for 3 hours, until the potatoes are tender.
7. Once the potatoes are tender, stir gently to coat them in the infused broth and herbs, then serve.

Chapter 7: Bold & Saucy

Chickpea Tikka Masala

Time: 3 hours 20 minutes	Serving Size: 2 bowls
Prep Time: 20 minutes	Cook Time: 3 hours

Each Serving Has:
Calories: 320, Carbohydrates: 44g, Saturated Fat: 2g, Protein: 13g, Fat: 10g, Sodium: 310mg, Potassium: 780mg, Fiber: 11g, Sugar: 7g, Vitamin C: 22mg, Calcium: 70mg, Iron: 4.2mg

Ingredients:
- 1 1/2 cups [255g] canned chickpeas, drained and rinsed
- 1/2 cup [120ml] canned light coconut milk
- 1 cup [240ml] canned crushed tomatoes (low-sodium)
- 1/4 cup [40g] chopped yellow onion
- 2 cloves garlic, minced
- 1 tsp grated fresh ginger
- 1 tbsp tomato paste (no salt added)
- 1 tbsp garam masala
- 1 tsp ground cumin
- 1/2 tsp ground turmeric
- 1/4 tsp smoked paprika
- 1/2 tsp sea salt
- 1 tbsp olive oil
- 1/4 cup [60ml] filtered water
- 1 tbsp chopped fresh cilantro

Directions:
1. Add the chickpeas, crushed tomatoes, and coconut milk to the slow cooker.
2. Mix in the chopped onion, minced garlic, and grated ginger.
3. Add the tomato paste, garam masala, cumin, turmeric, smoked paprika, and sea salt.
4. Drizzle olive oil evenly over the ingredients.
5. Pour in water and stir thoroughly until all ingredients are well combined.
6. Cover and cook on low for 3 hours, stirring once halfway through, until the chickpeas are tender and the sauce is thickened.
7. Garnish with the chopped fresh cilantro before serving.

Thai Red Lentil Curry

	Time: 3 hours 15 minutes		Serving Size: 2 bowls
	Prep Time: 15 minutes		Cook Time: 3 hours

Each Serving Has:
Calories: 298, Carbohydrates: 40g, Saturated Fat: 2g, Protein: 15g, Fat: 9g, Sodium: 320mg, Potassium: 860mg, Fiber: 10g, Sugar: 5g, Vitamin C: 10mg, Calcium: 50mg, Iron: 4.8mg

Ingredients:
- 3/4 cup [144g] red lentils, rinsed
- 1/2 cup [120ml] canned light coconut milk
- 1 cup [240ml] low-sodium vegetable broth
- 1/2 cup [80g] chopped red bell pepper
- 1/4 cup [40g] chopped yellow onion
- 1 tbsp Thai red curry paste (plant-based)
- 1 clove garlic, minced
- 1 tsp grated fresh ginger
- 1 tbsp fresh lime juice
- 1 tsp olive oil
- 1/4 tsp sea salt
- 1 tbsp chopped fresh cilantro

Directions:
1. Add the red lentils, coconut milk, and vegetable broth to the slow cooker.
2. Stir in the chopped bell pepper and onion.
3. Mix in the minced garlic, grated ginger, and Thai red curry paste.
4. Add the olive oil, fresh lime juice, and sea salt.
5. Stir thoroughly until all ingredients are well combined.
6. Cover and cook on low for 3 hours, stirring once halfway through, until the lentils are tender and the mixture is creamy.
7. Garnish with chopped fresh cilantro before serving.

Spicy Black Bean Chili

	Time: 3 hours 30 minutes		Serving Size: 2 bowls
	Prep Time: 15 minutes		Cook Time: 3 hours 15 minutes

Each Serving Has:
Calories: 310, Carbohydrates: 47g, Saturated Fat: 1g, Protein: 15g, Fat: 7g, Sodium: 360mg, Potassium: 890mg, Fiber: 14g, Sugar: 6g, Vitamin C: 24mg, Calcium: 80mg, Iron: 4.5mg

Ingredients:
- 1 1/2 cups [255g] canned black beans, drained and rinsed
- 1/2 cup [80g] chopped red bell pepper
- 1/4 cup [40g] chopped yellow onion
- 1 cup [240ml] canned crushed tomatoes (low-sodium)
- 1/2 cup [120ml] low-sodium vegetable broth
- 1 clove garlic, minced
- 1 tbsp tomato paste (no salt added)
- 1/2 tsp chipotle chili powder
- 1/2 tsp ground cumin
- 1/4 tsp smoked paprika
- 1/4 tsp sea salt
- 1 tbsp olive oil
- 1 tbsp chopped fresh parsley

Directions:
1. Add the black beans, crushed tomatoes, and vegetable broth to the slow cooker.
2. Stir in the chopped bell pepper and onion.
3. Add the minced garlic and tomato paste.
4. Sprinkle in the chili powder, cumin, smoked paprika, and sea salt.
5. Drizzle olive oil evenly over the mixture.
6. Stir thoroughly until all ingredients are well combined.
7. Cover and cook on low for 3 hours and 15 minutes, until the vegetables are tender and the mixture is thick and flavorful.
8. Garnish with chopped fresh parsley before serving.

Coconut Sweet Potato Curry

Time: 3 hours 20 minutes
Serving Size: 2 bowls
Prep Time: 20 minutes
Cook Time: 3 hours

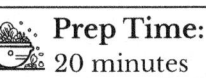

Each Serving Has:
Calories: 340, Carbohydrates: 49g, Saturated Fat: 4g, Protein: 7g, Fat: 12g, Sodium: 300mg, Potassium: 940mg, Fiber: 9g, Sugar: 11g, Vitamin C: 28mg, Calcium: 60mg, Iron: 3.9mg

Ingredients:
- 1 1/2 cups [210g] peeled and cubed sweet potatoes
- 1/2 cup [120ml] canned light coconut milk
- 1 cup [240ml] low-sodium vegetable broth
- 1/2 cup [80g] chopped red bell pepper
- 1/4 cup [40g] chopped red onion
- 1 tbsp red curry paste (plant-based)
- 1 clove garlic, minced
- 1 tsp grated fresh ginger
- 1 tbsp lime juice
- 1 tbsp olive oil
- 1/2 tsp ground coriander
- 1/4 tsp sea salt
- 1 tbsp chopped fresh basil

Directions:
1. Add the cubed sweet potatoes, vegetable broth, and coconut milk to the slow cooker.
2. Stir in the chopped bell pepper and onion.
3. Add the minced garlic, grated ginger, red curry paste, and lime juice.
4. Sprinkle in the coriander and sea salt.
5. Drizzle olive oil evenly over the mixture.
6. Stir gently until all ingredients are well combined.
7. Cover and cook on low for 3 hours, until the sweet potatoes are tender and the curry is creamy and fragrant.
8. Garnish with chopped fresh basil before serving.

Jamaican Jerk Veggie Stew

Time: 3 hours 25 minutes
Serving Size: 2 bowls
Prep Time: 25 minutes
Cook Time: 3 hours

Each Serving Has:
Calories: 305, Carbohydrates: 45g, Saturated Fat: 2g, Protein: 10g, Fat: 9g, Sodium: 330mg, Potassium: 910mg, Fiber: 11g, Sugar: 8g, Vitamin C: 36mg, Calcium: 70mg, Iron: 3.7mg

Ingredients:
- 1 cup [170g] canned kidney beans, drained and rinsed
- 1 cup [160g] chopped butternut squash
- 1/2 cup [80g] chopped red bell pepper
- 1/4 cup [40g] chopped green onion
- 1 clove garlic, minced
- 1 tsp grated fresh ginger
- 1 tbsp Jamaican jerk seasoning (salt-free)
- 1 tbsp tomato paste (no salt added)
- 1/2 cup [120ml] low-sodium vegetable broth
- 1/2 cup [120ml] canned light coconut milk
- 1 tbsp olive oil
- 1 tbsp fresh lime juice
- 1 tbsp chopped fresh parsley

Directions:
1. Add the kidney beans, chopped butternut squash, and bell pepper to the slow cooker.
2. Stir in the chopped green onion, minced garlic, and grated ginger.
3. Mix in the tomato paste and Jamaican jerk seasoning.
4. Pour in the vegetable broth and coconut milk.
5. Add the olive oil and fresh lime juice.
6. Stir thoroughly until all ingredients are well combined.
7. Cover and cook on low for 3 hours, until the squash is tender and the flavors are well blended.
8. Garnish with chopped fresh parsley before serving.

CHAPTER 7: BOLD & SAUCY

Butternut Chickpea Curry

⏰ Time: 3 hours 20 minutes	🍴 Serving Size: 2 bowls
🍚 Prep Time: 20 minutes	🍲 Cook Time: 3 hours

Each Serving Has:
Calories: 335, Carbohydrates: 50g, Saturated Fat: 3g, Protein: 11g, Fat: 10g, Sodium: 310mg, Potassium: 970mg, Fiber: 12g, Sugar: 8g, Vitamin C: 27mg, Calcium: 75mg, Iron: 4.1mg

Ingredients:
- 1 1/2 cups [255g] canned chickpeas, drained and rinsed
- 1 cup [160g] cubed butternut squash
- 1/2 cup [80g] chopped red bell pepper
- 1/4 cup [40g] chopped yellow onion
- 1 clove garlic, minced
- 1 tsp grated fresh ginger
- 1 tbsp curry powder
- 1 tbsp tomato paste (no salt added)
- 1/2 cup [120ml] canned light coconut milk
- 1/2 cup [120ml] low-sodium vegetable broth
- 1 tbsp olive oil
- 1/4 tsp sea salt
- 1 tbsp chopped fresh cilantro

Directions:
1. Add the chickpeas, cubed butternut squash, and chopped bell pepper to the slow cooker.
2. Stir in the chopped onion, minced garlic, and grated ginger.
3. Add the curry powder, tomato paste, and sea salt.
4. Pour in the coconut milk and vegetable broth.
5. Drizzle olive oil evenly over the mixture.
6. Stir thoroughly until all ingredients are well combined.
7. Cover and cook on low for 3 hours, until the squash is tender and the curry is rich and fragrant.
8. Garnish with chopped fresh cilantro before serving.

White Bean & Kale Chili

⏰ Time: 3 hours 20 minutes	🍴 Serving Size: 2 bowls
🍚 Prep Time: 20 minutes	🍲 Cook Time: 3 hours

Each Serving Has:
Calories: 295, Carbohydrates: 42g, Saturated Fat: 1g, Protein: 14g, Fat: 7g, Sodium: 280mg, Potassium: 920mg, Fiber: 12g, Sugar: 5g, Vitamin C: 31mg, Calcium: 110mg, Iron: 4.3mg

Ingredients:
- 1 1/2 cups [255g] canned white beans, drained and rinsed
- 1 cup [130g] chopped kale, stems removed
- 1/2 cup [80g] chopped carrots
- 1/4 cup [40g] chopped red onion
- 1 clove garlic, minced
- 1 tsp ground cumin
- 1/2 tsp smoked paprika
- 1 tbsp tomato paste (no salt added)
- 1 cup [240ml] low-sodium vegetable broth
- 1/2 cup [120ml] canned diced tomatoes
- 1 tbsp olive oil
- 1/4 tsp sea salt
- 1 tbsp chopped fresh parsley

Directions:
1. Add the white beans, chopped kale, carrots, and onion to the slow cooker.
2. Stir in the minced garlic, cumin, and smoked paprika.
3. Mix in the tomato paste and canned diced tomatoes.
4. Pour in the vegetable broth and drizzle in the olive oil.
5. Sprinkle in the sea salt and stir thoroughly until all ingredients are well combined.
6. Cover and cook on low for 3 hours, until the vegetables are tender and the stew is thick and flavorful.
7. Garnish with chopped fresh parsley before serving.

Ethiopian Berbere Lentils

Time: 3 hours 25 minutes
Serving Size: 2 bowls
Prep Time: 25 minutes
Cook Time: 3 hours

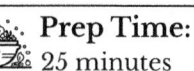

Each Serving Has:
Calories: 310, Carbohydrates: 46g, Saturated Fat: 1g, Protein: 16g, Fat: 6g, Sodium: 300mg, Potassium: 870mg, Fiber: 14g, Sugar: 4g, Vitamin C: 10mg, Calcium: 55mg, Iron: 5.2mg

Ingredients:
- 3/4 cup [144g] dry red lentils, rinsed
- 1 cup [240ml] low-sodium vegetable broth
- 1/2 cup [120ml] canned diced tomatoes (low-sodium)
- 1/4 cup [40g] chopped yellow onion
- 1 clove garlic, minced
- 1 tsp grated fresh ginger
- 1 tbsp tomato paste (no salt added)
- 1 tbsp berbere spice blend
- 1 tbsp olive oil
- 1/4 tsp sea salt
- 1 tbsp chopped fresh cilantro

Directions:
1. Add the red lentils, vegetable broth, and diced tomatoes to the slow cooker.
2. Stir in the chopped onion, minced garlic, and grated ginger.
3. Mix in the tomato paste and berbere spice blend.
4. Drizzle in the olive oil and sprinkle in the sea salt.
5. Stir thoroughly until all ingredients are well combined.
6. Cover and cook on low for 3 hours, until the lentils are tender and the flavors are well blended.
7. Garnish with chopped fresh cilantro before serving.

Creamy Cashew Cauliflower Curry

Time: 3 hours 30 minutes
Serving Size: 2 bowls
Prep Time: 30 minutes
Cook Time: 3 hours

Each Serving Has:
Calories: 345, Carbohydrates: 38g, Saturated Fat: 3g, Protein: 11g, Fat: 18g, Sodium: 290mg, Potassium: 910mg, Fiber: 9g, Sugar: 6g, Vitamin C: 52mg, Calcium: 65mg, Iron: 3.8mg

Ingredients:
- 1 1/2 cups [150g] cauliflower florets
- 1/4 cup [35g] raw cashews, soaked for 2 hours
- 1/2 cup [120ml] canned light coconut milk
- 1/2 cup [120ml] low-sodium vegetable broth
- 1/4 cup [40g] chopped white onion
- 1 clove garlic, minced
- 1 tsp grated fresh ginger
- 1 tbsp curry powder
- 1 tbsp fresh lime juice
- 1 tbsp tomato paste (no salt added)
- 1 tbsp olive oil
- 1/4 tsp sea salt
- 1 tbsp chopped fresh cilantro

Directions:
1. Add the cauliflower florets, chopped onion, and minced garlic to the slow cooker.
2. In a blender, combine the soaked cashews, coconut milk, and vegetable broth; blend until smooth.
3. Pour the cashew mixture over the vegetables into the slow cooker.
4. Stir in the grated ginger, curry powder, fresh lime juice, and tomato paste.
5. Add the olive oil and sea salt, and stir well to combine all ingredients evenly.
6. Cover and cook on low for 3 hours, until the cauliflower is tender and the sauce is creamy.
7. Garnish with chopped fresh cilantro before serving.

Smoky Tempeh Chili

Time: 3 hours 30 minutes
Serving Size: 2 bowls
Prep Time: 30 minutes
Cook Time: 3 hours

Each Serving Has:
Calories: 360, Carbohydrates: 34g, Saturated Fat: 2g, Protein: 20g, Fat: 18g, Sodium: 340mg, Potassium: 880mg, Fiber: 10g, Sugar: 6g, Vitamin C: 22mg, Calcium: 100mg, Iron: 4.9mg

Ingredients:
- 6 oz [170g] tempeh, crumbled
- 1/2 cup [80g] chopped red bell pepper
- 1/4 cup [40g] chopped red onion
- 1 cup [240ml] canned crushed tomatoes (low-sodium)
- 1/2 cup [120ml] low-sodium vegetable broth
- 1 clove garlic, minced
- 1 tbsp tomato paste (no salt added)
- 1 tsp smoked paprika
- 1/2 tsp ground cumin
- 1/2 tsp chili powder
- 1/4 tsp sea salt
- 1 tbsp olive oil
- 1 tbsp chopped fresh parsley

Directions:
1. Add the crumbled tempeh, chopped bell pepper, and onion to the slow cooker.
2. Stir in the minced garlic, crushed tomatoes, and tomato paste.
3. Add the vegetable broth, smoked paprika, cumin, chili powder, and sea salt.
4. Drizzle the olive oil over the mixture.
5. Stir thoroughly until all ingredients are well combined.
6. Cover and cook on low for 3 hours, until the flavors meld and the tempeh is tender.
7. Garnish with chopped fresh parsley before serving.

Green Thai Vegetable Curry

Time: 3 hours 25 minutes
Serving Size: 2 bowls
Prep Time: 25 minutes
Cook Time: 3 hours

Each Serving Has:
Calories: 320, Carbohydrates: 40g, Saturated Fat: 3g, Protein: 9g, Fat: 14g, Sodium: 310mg, Potassium: 920mg, Fiber: 8g, Sugar: 7g, Vitamin C: 36mg, Calcium: 75mg, Iron: 3.5mg

Ingredients:
- 1 cup [130g] broccoli florets
- 1 cup [160g] chopped zucchini
- 1/2 cup [80g] chopped red bell pepper
- 1/4 cup [40g] chopped yellow onion
- 1/2 cup [120ml] canned light coconut milk
- 1/2 cup [120ml] low-sodium vegetable broth
- 1 tbsp green curry paste (plant-based)
- 1 clove garlic, minced
- 1 tsp grated fresh ginger
- 1 tbsp fresh lime juice
- 1 tbsp olive oil
- 1/4 tsp sea salt
- 1 tbsp chopped fresh basil

Directions:
1. Add the broccoli florets, chopped zucchini, bell pepper, and onion to the slow cooker.
2. Stir in the minced garlic, grated ginger, and green curry paste.
3. Pour in the coconut milk and vegetable broth.
4. Add the lime juice, olive oil, and sea salt.
5. Mix everything together thoroughly until well combined.
6. Cover and cook on low for 3 hours, until the vegetables are tender and the flavors meld.
7. Garnish with chopped fresh basil before serving.

Chapter 8: Plant-Powered Grains

Cajun Black-Eyed Peas

Time: 3 hours 35 minutes	Serving Size: 2 bowls
Prep Time: 25 minutes	Cook Time: 3 hours 10 minutes

Each Serving Has:
Calories: 310, Carbohydrates: 42g, Saturated Fat: 1g, Protein: 15g, Fat: 7g, Sodium: 320mg, Potassium: 890mg, Fiber: 11g, Sugar: 5g, Vitamin C: 19mg, Calcium: 85mg, Iron: 4.2mg

Ingredients:
- 1 cup [190g] cooked black-eyed peas
- 1/2 cup [80g] chopped celery
- 1/2 cup [80g] chopped green bell pepper
- 1/4 cup [40g] chopped red onion
- 1 clove garlic, minced
- 1 tbsp tomato paste (no salt added)
- 1 tsp Cajun seasoning (salt-free)
- 1/2 tsp smoked paprika
- 1/2 tsp dried thyme
- 1/2 cup [120ml] low-sodium vegetable broth
- 1/2 cup [120ml] water
- 1 tbsp olive oil
- 1/4 tsp sea salt
- 1 tbsp chopped fresh parsley

Directions:
1. Add the cooked black-eyed peas, chopped celery, bell pepper, and onion to the slow cooker.
2. Stir in the minced garlic, tomato paste, Cajun seasoning, smoked paprika, and thyme.
3. Pour in the vegetable broth and water.
4. Add the olive oil and sprinkle with sea salt.
5. Stir thoroughly to combine all ingredients evenly.
6. Cover and cook on low for 3 hours and 10 minutes, until the vegetables are tender and the flavors meld.
7. Garnish with chopped fresh parsley before serving.

Ginger Turmeric Lentils

Time: 3 hours 20 minutes
Serving Size: 2 bowls
Prep Time: 20 minutes
Cook Time: 3 hours

Each Serving Has:
Calories: 295, Carbohydrates: 43g, Saturated Fat: 1g, Protein: 17g, Fat: 6g, Sodium: 270mg, Potassium: 910mg, Fiber: 13g, Sugar: 4g, Vitamin C: 8mg, Calcium: 50mg, Iron: 5.1mg

Ingredients:
- 3/4 cup [144g] dry green lentils, rinsed
- 1 cup [240ml] low-sodium vegetable broth
- 1/2 cup [120ml] water
- 1/4 cup [40g] chopped yellow onion
- 1 clove garlic, minced
- 1 tsp grated fresh ginger
- 1/2 tsp ground turmeric
- 1/4 tsp black pepper
- 1/2 tsp ground cumin
- 1 tbsp lemon juice
- 1 tbsp olive oil
- 1/4 tsp sea salt
- 1 tbsp chopped fresh cilantro

Directions:
1. Add the dry green lentils, vegetable broth, and water to the slow cooker.
2. Stir in the chopped onion, minced garlic, grated ginger, turmeric, and cumin.
3. Add the black pepper, sea salt, and lemon juice.
4. Drizzle in the olive oil and stir well.
5. Mix thoroughly to combine all the ingredients evenly.
6. Cover and cook on low for 3 hours, until the lentils are tender and the flavors are well blended.
7. Garnish with chopped fresh cilantro before serving.

Cuban Mojo Black Beans

Time: 3 hours 25 minutes
Serving Size: 2 bowls
Prep Time: 25 minutes
Cook Time: 3 hours

Each Serving Has:
Calories: 310, Carbohydrates: 44g, Saturated Fat: 1g, Protein: 15g, Fat: 7g, Sodium: 290mg, Potassium: 920mg, Fiber: 13g, Sugar: 5g, Vitamin C: 21mg, Calcium: 75mg, Iron: 4.5mg

Ingredients:
- 1 1/2 cups [255g] canned black beans, drained and rinsed
- 1/4 cup [40g] chopped white onion
- 1/2 cup [80g] chopped green bell pepper
- 2 cloves garlic, minced
- 1/2 cup [120ml] low-sodium vegetable broth
- 1/4 cup [60ml] orange juice
- 2 tbsp lime juice
- 1 tsp ground cumin
- 1/2 tsp dried oregano
- 1/4 tsp black pepper
- 1/4 tsp sea salt
- 1 tbsp olive oil
- 1 tbsp chopped fresh cilantro

Directions:
1. Add the black beans, chopped onion, and bell pepper to the slow cooker.
2. Stir in the minced garlic, cumin, oregano, black pepper, and sea salt.
3. Pour in the vegetable broth, orange juice, and lime juice.
4. Drizzle the olive oil over the mixture.
5. Stir thoroughly until all ingredients are well combined.
6. Cover and cook on low for 3 hours, until the vegetables are tender and the flavors have melded.
7. Garnish with chopped fresh cilantro before serving.

Brown Rice & Pinto Bowl

Time: 3 hours 30 minutes
Serving Size: 2 bowls
Prep Time: 20 minutes
Cook Time: 3 hours 10 minutes

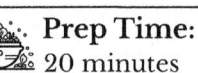

Each Serving Has:
Calories: 340, Carbohydrates: 52g, Saturated Fat: 1g, Protein: 13g, Fat: 8g, Sodium: 280mg, Potassium: 900mg, Fiber: 10g, Sugar: 4g, Vitamin C: 15mg, Calcium: 60mg, Iron: 3.9mg

Ingredients:
- 3/4 cup [135g] cooked brown rice
- 1 1/2 cups [255g] canned pinto beans, drained and rinsed
- 1/2 cup [80g] chopped tomato
- 1/4 cup [40g] chopped red onion
- 1/2 cup [120ml] low-sodium vegetable broth
- 1 clove garlic, minced
- 1 tbsp tomato paste (no salt added)
- 1 tsp ground cumin
- 1/4 tsp sea salt
- 1/2 tsp smoked paprika
- 1 tbsp fresh lime juice
- 1 tbsp olive oil
- 1 tbsp chopped fresh cilantro

Directions:
1. Add the cooked rice, pinto beans, chopped tomato, and onion to the slow cooker.
2. Stir in the minced garlic, tomato paste, cumin, sea salt, and smoked paprika.
3. Pour in the vegetable broth and lime juice.
4. Drizzle the olive oil over the mixture.
5. Stir thoroughly to combine all ingredients.
6. Cover and cook on low for 3 hours and 10 minutes, until the flavors are well blended and the dish is heated through.
7. Garnish with chopped fresh cilantro before serving.

Lemony Farro and Fava Beans

Time: 3 hours 25 minutes
Serving Size: 2 bowls
Prep Time: 25 minutes
Cook Time: 3 hours

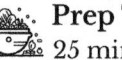

Each Serving Has:
Calories: 330, Carbohydrates: 48g, Saturated Fat: 1g, Protein: 14g, Fat: 9g, Sodium: 260mg, Potassium: 920mg, Fiber: 11g, Sugar: 3g, Vitamin C: 18mg, Calcium: 60mg, Iron: 3.6mg

Ingredients:
- 3/4 cup [120g] cooked farro
- 1 cup [170g] shelled fava beans
- 1/2 cup [80g] chopped zucchini
- 1/4 cup [40g] chopped red onion
- 1 clove garlic, minced
- 1/2 cup [120ml] low-sodium vegetable broth
- 2 tbsp lemon juice
- 1 tsp lemon zest
- 1/2 tsp dried thyme
- 1/4 tsp sea salt
- 1 tbsp olive oil
- 1 tbsp chopped fresh parsley

Directions:
1. Add the cooked farro, shelled fava beans, chopped zucchini, and onion to the slow cooker.
2. Stir in the minced garlic, thyme, lemon zest, and sea salt.
3. Pour in the vegetable broth and lemon juice.
4. Drizzle the olive oil over the mixture.
5. Stir thoroughly until all ingredients are well combined.
6. Cover and cook on low for 3 hours, until the vegetables are tender and the flavors are well blended.
7. Garnish with chopped fresh parsley before serving.

Smoky Cannellini with Spinach

Time: 3 hours 20 minutes
Serving Size: 2 bowls
Prep Time: 20 minutes
Cook Time: 3 hours

Each Serving Has:
Calories: 315, Carbohydrates: 41g, Saturated Fat: 1g, Protein: 16g, Fat: 9g, Sodium: 270mg, Potassium: 940mg, Fiber: 12g, Sugar: 3g, Vitamin C: 19mg, Calcium: 110mg, Iron: 4.6mg

Ingredients:
- 1 1/2 cups [255g] canned cannellini beans, drained and rinsed
- 1 cup [30g] fresh spinach, chopped
- 1/2 cup [80g] chopped carrot
- 1/4 cup [40g] chopped white onion
- 1 clove garlic, minced
- 1/2 cup [120ml] low-sodium vegetable broth
- 1 tbsp tomato paste (no salt added)
- 1 tsp smoked paprika
- 1/2 tsp dried rosemary
- 1 tbsp olive oil
- 1/4 tsp sea salt
- 1 tbsp chopped fresh parsley

Directions:
1. Add the cannellini beans, chopped spinach, carrot, and onion to the slow cooker.
2. Stir in the minced garlic, tomato paste, smoked paprika, and rosemary.
3. Pour in the vegetable broth and drizzle the olive oil over the mixture.
4. Add the sea salt and stir thoroughly to combine all ingredients evenly.
5. Cover and cook on low for 3 hours, until the vegetables are tender and the flavors are well blended.
6. Garnish with chopped fresh parsley before serving.

Savory Chickpeas with Wild Rice

Time: 3 hours 30 minutes
Serving Size: 2 bowls
Prep Time: 20 minutes
Cook Time: 3 hours 10 minutes

Each Serving Has:
Calories: 340, Carbohydrates: 48g, Saturated Fat: 1g, Protein: 15g, Fat: 9g, Sodium: 290mg, Potassium: 930mg, Fiber: 12g, Sugar: 4g, Vitamin C: 16mg, Calcium: 70mg, Iron: 4.2mg

Ingredients:
- 3/4 cup [125g] cooked wild rice
- 1 1/2 cups [255g] canned chickpeas, drained and rinsed
- 1/2 cup [80g] chopped red bell pepper
- 1/4 cup [40g] chopped yellow onion
- 1 clove garlic, minced
- 1/2 cup [120ml] low-sodium vegetable broth
- 1 tbsp tomato paste (no salt added)
- 1 tsp ground coriander
- 1/2 tsp ground cumin
- 1/4 tsp black pepper
- 1/4 tsp sea salt
- 1 tbsp olive oil
- 1 tbsp chopped fresh parsley

Directions:
1. Add the cooked rice, chickpeas, chopped bell pepper, and onion to the slow cooker.
2. Stir in the minced garlic, tomato paste, coriander, cumin, black pepper, and sea salt.
3. Pour in the vegetable broth and drizzle the olive oil over the mixture.
4. Mix all ingredients thoroughly to combine the flavors.
5. Cover and cook on low for 3 hours and 10 minutes, until the vegetables are tender and the flavors are well blended.
6. Stir gently and garnish with the chopped fresh parsley before serving.

Barley and Vegetable Pilaf

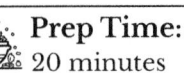

Time: 3 hours 30 minutes
Serving Size: 2 bowls
Prep Time: 20 minutes
Cook Time: 3 hours 10 minutes

Each Serving Has:
Calories: 325, Carbohydrates: 50g, Saturated Fat: 1g, Protein: 10g, Fat: 8g, Sodium: 260mg, Potassium: 880mg, Fiber: 9g, Sugar: 5g, Vitamin C: 20mg, Calcium: 55mg, Iron: 3.4mg

Ingredients:
- 3/4 cup [135g] cooked pearl barley
- 1/2 cup [80g] chopped carrot
- 1/2 cup [80g] chopped zucchini
- 1/4 cup [40g] chopped red onion
- 1 clove garlic, minced
- 1 tbsp tomato paste (no salt added)
- 1/2 tsp dried thyme
- 1/4 tsp black pepper
- 1/4 tsp sea salt
- 1/2 cup [120ml] low-sodium vegetable broth
- 1/2 cup [120ml] water
- 1 tbsp olive oil
- 1 tbsp chopped fresh dill

Directions:
1. Add the cooked pearl barley, chopped carrot, zucchini, and onion to the slow cooker.
2. Stir in the minced garlic, tomato paste, thyme, black pepper, and sea salt.
3. Pour in the vegetable broth and water.
4. Drizzle the olive oil over the mixture.
5. Mix everything thoroughly until well combined.
6. Cover and cook on low for 3 hours and 10 minutes, until the vegetables are tender and the flavors are well blended.
7. Garnish with the chopped fresh dill before serving.

Cajun Red Beans and Rice

Time: 3 hours 30 minutes
Serving Size: 2 bowls
Prep Time: 20 minutes
Cook Time: 3 hours 10 minutes

Each Serving Has:
Calories: 345, Carbohydrates: 52g, Saturated Fat: 1g, Protein: 14g, Fat: 8g, Sodium: 300mg, Potassium: 940mg, Fiber: 12g, Sugar: 4g, Vitamin C: 17mg, Calcium: 70mg, Iron: 4.4mg

Ingredients:
- 3/4 cup [135g] cooked brown rice
- 1 1/2 cups [255g] canned red kidney beans, drained and rinsed
- 1/2 cup [80g] chopped green bell pepper
- 1/4 cup [40g] chopped celery
- 1/4 cup [40g] chopped red onion
- 1 clove garlic, minced
- 1 tbsp tomato paste (no salt added)
- 1 tsp Cajun seasoning (salt-free)
- 1/2 tsp smoked paprika
- 1/4 tsp dried thyme
- 1/4 tsp sea salt
- 1/2 cup [120ml] low-sodium vegetable broth
- 1 tbsp olive oil
- 1 tbsp chopped fresh parsley

Directions:
1. Add the cooked brown rice, kidney beans, chopped bell pepper, celery, and onion to the slow cooker.
2. Stir in the minced garlic, tomato paste, Cajun seasoning, smoked paprika, thyme, and sea salt.
3. Pour in the vegetable broth and drizzle the olive oil over the mixture.
4. Stir thoroughly until all ingredients are fully combined.
5. Cover and cook on low for 3 hours and 10 minutes, until the vegetables are tender and the flavors are well blended.
6. Stir gently and garnish with the chopped fresh parsley before serving.

CHAPTER 8: PLANT-POWERED GRAINS ◊ 61

Mexican-Spiced Lentil Medley

⏱ **Time:** 3 hours 30 minutes	🍽 **Serving Size:** 2 bowls
🥣 **Prep Time:** 20 minutes	🍲 **Cook Time:** 3 hours 10 minutes

Each Serving Has:
Calories: 335, Carbohydrates: 49g, Saturated Fat: 1g, Protein: 17g, Fat: 7g, Sodium: 290mg, Potassium: 960mg, Fiber: 13g, Sugar: 5g, Vitamin C: 19mg, Calcium: 65mg, Iron: 4.8mg

Ingredients:
- 3/4 cup [144g] dry brown lentils, rinsed
- 1/2 cup [80g] chopped red bell pepper
- 1/2 cup [80g] chopped zucchini
- 1/4 cup [40g] chopped red onion
- 1 clove garlic, minced
- 1 tbsp tomato paste (no salt added)
- 1 tsp ground cumin
- 1/2 tsp chili powder
- 1/2 tsp smoked paprika
- 1/4 tsp sea salt
- 1/2 cup [120ml] low-sodium vegetable broth
- 1/2 cup [120ml] water
- 1 tbsp olive oil
- 1 tbsp chopped fresh cilantro

Directions:
1. Add the brown lentils, chopped bell pepper, zucchini, and onion to the slow cooker.
2. Stir in the minced garlic, tomato paste, cumin, chili powder, smoked paprika, and sea salt.
3. Pour in the vegetable broth and water.
4. Drizzle the olive oil over the mixture.
5. Stir thoroughly until all ingredients are well mixed.
6. Cover and cook on low for 3 hours and 10 minutes, until the lentils are tender and the flavors are well blended.
7. Garnish with the chopped fresh cilantro before serving.

Sun-Dried Tomato Quinoa

⏱ **Time:** 3 hours 20 minutes	🍽 **Serving Size:** 2 bowls
🥣 **Prep Time:** 20 minutes	🍲 **Cook Time:** 3 hours

Each Serving Has:
Calories: 325, Carbohydrates: 44g, Saturated Fat: 1g, Protein: 13g, Fat: 10g, Sodium: 270mg, Potassium: 850mg, Fiber: 8g, Sugar: 4g, Vitamin C: 14mg, Calcium: 55mg, Iron: 4.1mg

Ingredients:
- 3/4 cup [128g] uncooked quinoa, rinsed
- 1/4 cup [40g] chopped sun-dried tomatoes (not oil-packed)
- 1/2 cup [80g] chopped red bell pepper
- 1/4 cup [40g] chopped white onion
- 1 clove garlic, minced
- 1 tsp dried basil
- 1/4 tsp black pepper
- 1/4 tsp sea salt
- 1/2 cup [120ml] low-sodium vegetable broth
- 1/2 cup [120ml] water
- 1 tbsp olive oil
- 1 tbsp chopped fresh parsley

Directions:
1. Add the rinsed quinoa, chopped sun-dried tomatoes, bell pepper, and onion to the slow cooker.
2. Stir in the minced garlic, basil, black pepper, and sea salt.
3. Pour in the vegetable broth and water.
4. Drizzle the olive oil over the mixture and stir thoroughly.
5. Combine all ingredients until evenly mixed.
6. Cover and cook on low for 3 hours, until the quinoa is tender and the flavors are well combined.
7. Garnish with the chopped fresh parsley before serving.

Chapter 9: Tangle-Free Twists

Creamy Vegan Mac & Peas

Time: 3 hours 20 minutes	Serving Size: 2 bowls
Prep Time: 20 minutes	Cook Time: 3 hours

Each Serving Has:
Calories: 355, Carbohydrates: 48g, Saturated Fat: 2g, Protein: 14g, Fat: 12g, Sodium: 320mg, Potassium: 780mg, Fiber: 9g, Sugar: 5g, Vitamin C: 11mg, Calcium: 60mg, Iron: 3.9mg

Ingredients:
- 1 cup [170g] whole wheat elbow macaroni
- 1/2 cup [80g] green peas (frozen or fresh)
- 1/4 cup [40g] chopped yellow onion
- 1 clove garlic, minced
- 1/2 cup [120ml] unsweetened almond milk
- 1/4 cup [60ml] low-sodium vegetable broth
- 2 tbsp nutritional yeast
- 1 tbsp lemon juice
- 1 tbsp olive oil
- 1/2 tsp ground mustard
- 1/4 tsp sea salt
- 1/4 tsp black pepper
- 1 tbsp chopped fresh parsley

Directions:
1. Add the elbow macaroni, green peas, chopped onion, and minced garlic to the slow cooker.
2. Pour in the almond milk and vegetable broth.
3. Stir in the nutritional yeast, lemon juice, mustard, sea salt, and black pepper.
4. Drizzle the olive oil over the mixture.
5. Stir thoroughly until all ingredients are well combined.
6. Cover and cook on low for 3 hours, until the pasta is tender and the mixture is creamy.
7. Garnish with the chopped fresh parsley before serving.

Garlic Alfredo Zucchini Pasta

⏰ **Time:** 3 hours 20 minutes	🍴 **Serving Size:** 2 bowls
🍲 **Prep Time:** 20 minutes	🍲 **Cook Time:** 3 hours

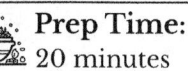

Each Serving Has:
Calories: 280, Carbohydrates: 22g, Saturated Fat: 2g, Protein: 9g, Fat: 18g, Sodium: 240mg, Potassium: 790mg, Fiber: 6g, Sugar: 7g, Vitamin C: 23mg, Calcium: 55mg, Iron: 2.8mg

Ingredients:
- 2 medium zucchini, spiralized (about 3 cups [375g])
- 1/4 cup [40g] chopped white onion
- 2 cloves garlic, minced
- 1/2 cup [120ml] unsweetened almond milk
- 1/4 cup [30g] raw cashews, soaked for 2 hours
- 1 tbsp lemon juice
- 2 tbsp nutritional yeast
- 1 tbsp olive oil
- 1/4 tsp ground nutmeg
- 1/4 tsp sea salt
- 1/4 tsp black pepper
- 1 tbsp chopped fresh basil

Directions:
1. Add the spiralized zucchini and chopped onion to the slow cooker.
2. In a blender, combine the almond milk, soaked cashews, lemon juice, and nutritional yeast.
3. Blend until creamy, then pour the mixture over the zucchini and onion.
4. Stir in the minced garlic, nutmeg, sea salt, and black pepper.
5. Drizzle the olive oil over the mixture and stir to combine.
6. Cover and cook on low for 3 hours, until the zucchini is tender and the sauce is creamy.
7. Garnish with chopped fresh basil before serving.

Spaghetti Squash Primavera

⏰ **Time:** 3 hours 30 minutes	🍴 **Serving Size:** 2 bowls
🍲 **Prep Time:** 20 minutes	🍲 **Cook Time:** 3 hours 10 minutes

Each Serving Has:
Calories: 295, Carbohydrates: 36g, Saturated Fat: 1g, Protein: 8g, Fat: 14g, Sodium: 250mg, Potassium: 870mg, Fiber: 9g, Sugar: 10g, Vitamin C: 42mg, Calcium: 60mg, Iron: 3.2mg

Ingredients:
- 1 small spaghetti squash (about 2 1/2 cups [475g])
- 1/2 cup [80g] chopped zucchini
- 1/2 cup [80g] chopped red bell pepper
- 1/4 cup [40g] chopped red onion
- 1 clove garlic, minced
- 1/2 cup [120ml] low-sodium vegetable broth
- 1 tbsp lemon juice
- 1 tbsp olive oil
- 1/2 tsp dried Italian seasoning
- 1/4 tsp sea salt
- 1/4 tsp black pepper
- 1 tbsp chopped fresh parsley

Directions:
1. Cut the spaghetti squash in half, scoop out the seeds, and place the squash cut side down in the slow cooker.
2. Add the chopped zucchini, bell pepper, onion, and minced garlic around the squash.
3. Pour in the vegetable broth and drizzle with olive oil.
4. Sprinkle with lemon juice, Italian seasoning, sea salt, and black pepper.
5. Cover and cook on low for 3 hours and 10 minutes, until the squash is tender.
6. Carefully remove the squash and shred it with a fork.
7. Toss the shredded squash with the vegetables in the slow cooker.
8. Garnish with chopped fresh parsley before serving.

Slow-Cooked Lasagna Roll-Ups

🕐 Time: 3 hours 30 minutes	🍴 Serving Size: 2 rolls
🍲 Prep Time: 20 minutes	🍳 Cook Time: 3 hours 10 minutes

Each Serving Has:
Calories: 370, Carbohydrates: 47g, Saturated Fat: 2g, Protein: 14g, Fat: 13g, Sodium: 320mg, Potassium: 780mg, Fiber: 8g, Sugar: 6g, Vitamin C: 15mg, Calcium: 75mg, Iron: 4.1mg

Ingredients:
- 4 whole wheat lasagna noodles, cooked
- 1/2 cup [120g] mashed firm tofu
- 1/2 cup [80g] chopped spinach
- 1/4 cup [40g] chopped zucchini
- 1 clove garlic, minced
- 1/2 tsp dried basil
- 1/4 tsp dried oregano
- 1/4 tsp sea salt
- 1/4 tsp black pepper
- 1 cup [240ml] low-sodium marinara sauce
- 1 tbsp olive oil
- 1 tbsp nutritional yeast
- 1 tbsp chopped fresh basil

Directions:
1. In a bowl, combine the mashed tofu, chopped spinach, zucchini, minced garlic, basil, oregano, sea salt, black pepper, and nutritional yeast.
2. Spread the filling evenly onEach cooked lasagna noodle and roll them up.
3. Add half of the marinara sauce to the bottom of the slow cooker.
4. Place the lasagna rolls seam-side down on top of the sauce.
5. Pour the remaining marinara sauce over the rolls and drizzle with olive oil.
6. Cover and cook on low for 3 hours and 10 minutes, until the rolls are heated through.
7. Garnish with chopped fresh basil before serving.

Thai Peanut Noodle Bowl

🕐 Time: 3 hours 20 minutes	🍴 Serving Size: 2 bowls
🍲 Prep Time: 20 minutes	🍳 Cook Time: 3 hours

Each Serving Has:
Calories: 385, Carbohydrates: 49g, Saturated Fat: 3g, Protein: 15g, Fat: 16g, Sodium: 340mg, Potassium: 780mg, Fiber: 7g, Sugar: 6g, Vitamin C: 20mg, Calcium: 60mg, Iron: 3.5mg

Ingredients:
- 4 oz [113g] whole wheat spaghetti, broken in half
- 1/2 cup [80g] shredded carrots
- 1/2 cup [80g] chopped red bell pepper
- 1/4 cup [40g] chopped green onion
- 2 tbsp natural peanut butter
- 1 tbsp low-sodium soy sauce
- 1 tbsp lime juice
- 1 tsp maple syrup
- 1 clove garlic, minced
- 1/2 tsp grated fresh ginger
- 1/2 cup [120ml] low-sodium vegetable broth
- 1/2 cup [120ml] water
- 1 tbsp olive oil
- 1 tbsp chopped fresh cilantro

Directions:
1. Add the broken spaghetti, shredded carrots, chopped bell pepper, and green onion to the slow cooker.
2. In a bowl, whisk together the peanut butter, soy sauce, lime juice, maple syrup, minced garlic, and grated ginger.
3. Pour the peanut mixture over the noodles and vegetables in the slow cooker.
4. Add the vegetable broth and water to the slow cooker.
5. Drizzle the olive oil over the mixture and stir gently to combine.
6. Cover and cook on low for 3 hours, until the noodles are tender and the flavors have melded.
7. Garnish with chopped fresh cilantro before serving.

CHAPTER 9: TANGLE-FREE TWISTS

Mushroom Stroganoff Pasta

Time: 3 hours 30 minutes
Serving Size: 2 bowls
Prep Time: 20 minutes
Cook Time: 3 hours 10 minutes

Each Serving Has:
Calories: 360, Carbohydrates: 46g, Saturated Fat: 2g, Protein: 13g, Fat: 14g, Sodium: 310mg, Potassium: 790mg, Fiber: 7g, Sugar: 4g, Vitamin C: 9mg, Calcium: 50mg, Iron: 3.8mg

Ingredients:
- 4 oz [113g] whole wheat rotini pasta
- 1 1/2 cups [135g] sliced cremini mushrooms
- 1/4 cup [40g] chopped yellow onion
- 1 clove garlic, minced
- 1/2 cup [120ml] unsweetened almond milk
- 1/4 cup [60ml] low-sodium vegetable broth
- 2 tbsp raw cashews, soaked for 2 hours
- 1 tbsp nutritional yeast
- 1 tbsp lemon juice
- 1 tbsp olive oil
- 1/2 tsp dried thyme
- 1/4 tsp sea salt
- 1/4 tsp black pepper
- 1 tbsp chopped fresh parsley

Directions:
1. Add the rotini pasta, sliced mushrooms, chopped onion, and minced garlic to the slow cooker.
2. In a blender, combine the almond milk, soaked cashews, lemon juice, nutritional yeast, and vegetable broth.
3. Blend until smooth and creamy, then pour the mixture into the slow cooker.
4. Stir in the thyme, sea salt, black pepper, and olive oil.
5. Mix everything together until well combined.
6. Cover and cook on low for 3 hours and 10 minutes, until the pasta is tender and the sauce is creamy.
7. Garnish with chopped fresh parsley before serving.

Butternut Squash Shells

Time: 3 hours 30 minutes
Serving Size: 2 servings
Prep Time: 20 minutes
Cook Time: 3 hours 10 minutes

Each Serving Has:
Calories: 340, Carbohydrates: 51g, Saturated Fat: 2g, Protein: 11g, Fat: 11g, Sodium: 270mg, Potassium: 880mg, Fiber: 8g, Sugar: 6g, Vitamin C: 28mg, Calcium: 65mg, Iron: 3.9mg

Ingredients:
- 4 oz [113g] whole wheat pasta shells
- 1 1/2 cups [210g] cubed butternut squash
- 1/4 cup [40g] chopped yellow onion
- 1 clove garlic, minced
- 1/2 cup [120ml] unsweetened almond milk
- 1/4 cup [60ml] low-sodium vegetable broth
- 2 tbsp raw cashews, soaked for 2 hours
- 1 tbsp nutritional yeast
- 1 tbsp lemon juice
- 1/2 tsp ground nutmeg
- 1/4 tsp sea salt
- 1/4 tsp black pepper
- 1 tbsp olive oil
- 1 tbsp chopped fresh sage

Directions:
1. Add the pasta shells, cubed butternut squash, chopped onion, and minced garlic to the slow cooker.
2. In a blender, combine the almond milk, vegetable broth, soaked cashews, lemon juice, and nutritional yeast.
3. Blend until smooth and creamy, then pour the mixture over the squash and pasta in the slow cooker.
4. Stir in the ground nutmeg, sea salt, black pepper, and olive oil.
5. Mix thoroughly until all ingredients are evenly combined.
6. Cover and cook on low for 3 hours and 10 minutes, until the squash is tender and the flavors meld together.
7. Garnish with chopped fresh sage before serving.

Lemon Garlic Orzo

Time: 3 hours 20 minutes
Serving Size: 2 bowls
Prep Time: 20 minutes
Cook Time: 3 hours

Each Serving Has:
Calories: 330, Carbohydrates: 48g, Saturated Fat: 1g, Protein: 10g, Fat: 11g, Sodium: 260mg, Potassium: 720mg, Fiber: 6g, Sugar: 3g, Vitamin C: 22mg, Calcium: 50mg, Iron: 3.1mg

Ingredients:
- 3/4 cup [130g] dry orzo pasta
- 1/2 cup [80g] chopped asparagus
- 1/4 cup [40g] chopped shallots
- 1 clove garlic, minced
- 1 tbsp lemon zest
- 2 tbsp lemon juice
- 1/2 cup [120ml] low-sodium vegetable broth
- 1/2 cup [120ml] water
- 1 tbsp olive oil
- 1/4 tsp sea salt
- 1/4 tsp black pepper
- 1 tbsp chopped fresh dill

Directions:
1. Add the orzo pasta, chopped asparagus, shallots, and minced garlic to the slow cooker.
2. Stir in the lemon zest, lemon juice, sea salt, and black pepper.
3. Pour in the vegetable broth and water.
4. Drizzle the olive oil over the mixture.
5. Stir everything well until all ingredients are evenly combined.
6. Cover and cook on low for 3 hours, until the orzo is tender and the flavors have melded together.
7. Garnish with chopped fresh dill before serving.

Teriyaki Udon Stir-Fry

Time: 3 hours 20 minutes
Serving Size: 2 bowls
Prep Time: 20 minutes
Cook Time: 3 hours

Each Serving Has:
Calories: 360, Carbohydrates: 54g, Saturated Fat: 1g, Protein: 12g, Fat: 10g, Sodium: 340mg, Potassium: 710mg, Fiber: 6g, Sugar: 7g, Vitamin C: 18mg, Calcium: 45mg, Iron: 3.5mg

Ingredients:
- 6 oz [170g] fresh udon noodles
- 1/2 cup [80g] chopped broccoli florets
- 1/2 cup [80g] sliced bell pepper
- 1/4 cup [40g] chopped carrots
- 1/4 cup [60ml] low-sodium teriyaki sauce
- 2 tbsp low-sodium vegetable broth
- 1 tbsp rice vinegar
- 1 tsp maple syrup
- 1 clove garlic, minced
- 1/2 tsp grated fresh ginger
- 1 tbsp sesame oil
- 1 tbsp chopped green onion

Directions:
1. Add the udon noodles, chopped broccoli florets, carrots, and sliced bell pepper to the slow cooker.
2. Stir in the teriyaki sauce, vegetable broth, rice vinegar, and maple syrup.
3. Add the minced garlic, grated ginger, and sesame oil to the mixture.
4. Stir everything well until all ingredients are evenly combined.
5. Cover and cook on low for 3 hours, until the vegetables are tender and the noodles are fully cooked.
6. Toss the noodles gently and garnish with the chopped green onion before serving.

CHAPTER 9: TANGLE-FREE TWISTS

Creamy Tomato Penne Bake

Time: 3 hours 30 minutes	Serving Size: 2 servings
Prep Time: 20 minutes	Cook Time: 3 hours 10 minutes

Each Serving Has:
Calories: 370, Carbohydrates: 52g, Saturated Fat: 2g, Protein: 13g, Fat: 12g, Sodium: 330mg, Potassium: 750mg, Fiber: 8g, Sugar: 6g, Vitamin C: 14mg, Calcium: 60mg, Iron: 4.2mg

Ingredients:
- 1 cup [170g] whole wheat penne pasta
- 1/2 cup [120ml] canned crushed tomatoes (low-sodium)
- 1/4 cup [60ml] unsweetened almond milk
- 1/4 cup [40g] chopped yellow onion
- 1/2 cup [80g] chopped zucchini
- 1 clove garlic, minced
- 2 tbsp raw cashews, soaked for 2 hours
- 1 tbsp tomato paste (no salt added)
- 1 tbsp nutritional yeast
- 1 tbsp olive oil
- 1/2 tsp dried oregano
- 1/4 tsp sea salt
- 1/4 tsp black pepper
- 1 tbsp chopped fresh basil

Directions:
1. Add the penne pasta, chopped onion, zucchini, minced garlic, and crushed tomatoes to the slow cooker.
2. In a blender, combine the almond milk, soaked cashews, tomato paste, and nutritional yeast.
3. Blend until smooth, then pour the creamy mixture over the pasta and vegetables.
4. Stir in the oregano, sea salt, black pepper, and olive oil.
5. Mix everything well to combine the flavors evenly.
6. Cover and cook on low for 3 hours and 10 minutes, until the pasta is tender and the sauce is creamy.
7. Garnish with chopped fresh basil before serving.

Pesto Pasta with White Beans

Time: 3 hours 20 minutes	Serving Size: 2 bowls
Prep Time: 20 minutes	Cook Time: 3 hours

Each Serving Has:
Calories: 375, Carbohydrates: 49g, Saturated Fat: 2g, Protein: 15g, Fat: 14g, Sodium: 320mg, Potassium: 760mg, Fiber: 9g, Sugar: 4g, Vitamin C: 12mg, Calcium: 65mg, Iron: 4.3mg

Ingredients:
- 1 cup [170g] whole wheat fusilli pasta
- 3/4 cup [130g] canned white beans, drained and rinsed
- 1/2 cup [80g] chopped cherry tomatoes
- 1/4 cup [40g] chopped zucchini
- 1/4 cup [60ml] low-sodium vegetable broth
- 2 tbsp fresh basil leaves
- 2 tbsp raw cashews
- 1 tbsp lemon juice
- 1 clove garlic, minced
- 1 tbsp olive oil
- 1 tbsp nutritional yeast
- 1/4 tsp sea salt
- 1/4 tsp black pepper
- 1 tbsp chopped fresh basil

Directions:
1. Add the fusilli pasta, white beans, chopped cherry tomatoes, and zucchini to the slow cooker.
2. In a blender, combine the basil leaves, raw cashews, lemon juice, minced garlic, olive oil, nutritional yeast, vegetable broth, sea salt, and black pepper.
3. Blend until smooth to create a pesto sauce.
4. Pour the pesto sauce over the pasta mixture in the slow cooker.
5. Stir well until everything is evenly coated.
6. Cover and cook on low for 3 hours, until the pasta is tender and the flavors have melded together.
7. Garnish with chopped fresh basil before serving.

Chapter 10: Purely Plant-Based

Braised Tofu with Root Veggies

Time: 3 hours 30 minutes	Serving Size: 2 bowls
Prep Time: 20 minutes	Cook Time: 3 hours 10 minutes

Each Serving Has:
Calories: 340, Carbohydrates: 38g, Saturated Fat: 1g, Protein: 17g, Fat: 13g, Sodium: 290mg, Potassium: 910mg, Fiber: 8g, Sugar: 7g, Vitamin C: 22mg, Calcium: 150mg, Iron: 4.6mg

Ingredients:
- 6 oz [170g] extra-firm tofu, pressed and cubed
- 1/2 cup [80g] chopped carrots
- 1/2 cup [80g] cubed parsnips
- 1/2 cup [80g] cubed sweet potatoes
- 1/4 cup [40g] chopped white onion
- 1 clove garlic, minced
- 1 tbsp low-sodium soy sauce
- 1/2 cup [120ml] low-sodium vegetable broth
- 1 tbsp balsamic vinegar
- 1 tbsp olive oil
- 1/2 tsp dried thyme
- 1/4 tsp black pepper
- 1 tbsp chopped fresh parsley

Directions:
1. Add the cubed tofu, chopped carrots, onion, cubed parsnips, and sweet potatoes to the slow cooker.
2. Stir in the minced garlic, thyme, and black pepper.
3. In a small bowl, mix the soy sauce, balsamic vinegar, and vegetable broth.
4. Pour the liquid mixture over the tofu and vegetables.
5. Drizzle the olive oil over everything and stir gently to combine.
6. Cover and cook on low for 3 hours and 10 minutes, until the vegetables are tender and the flavors have melded together.
7. Garnish with the chopped fresh parsley before serving.

Tempeh and Broccoli Stir Bowl

Time: 3 hours 20 minutes
Serving Size: 2 bowls
Prep Time: 20 minutes
Cook Time: 3 hours

Each Serving Has:
Calories: 355, Carbohydrates: 30g, Saturated Fat: 2g, Protein: 20g, Fat: 18g, Sodium: 310mg, Potassium: 760mg, Fiber: 7g, Sugar: 5g, Vitamin C: 35mg, Calcium: 110mg, Iron: 4.8mg

Ingredients:
- 6 oz [170g] tempeh, cubed
- 1 cup [130g] broccoli florets
- 1/4 cup [40g] sliced red bell pepper
- 1/4 cup [40g] chopped yellow onion
- 1 clove garlic, minced
- 2 tbsp low-sodium soy sauce
- 1 tbsp maple syrup
- 1 tbsp rice vinegar
- 1/2 cup [120ml] low-sodium vegetable broth
- 1 tbsp olive oil
- 1/2 tsp grated fresh ginger
- 1/4 tsp black pepper
- 1 tbsp chopped green onion

Directions:
1. Add the cubed tempeh, broccoli florets, sliced bell pepper, and chopped onion to the slow cooker.
2. Stir in the minced garlic, grated ginger, and black pepper.
3. In a bowl, whisk together the soy sauce, maple syrup, rice vinegar, and vegetable broth.
4. Pour the sauce over the tempeh and vegetables in the slow cooker.
5. Drizzle the olive oil over the mixture and stir well to combine.
6. Cover and cook on low for 3 hours, until the tempeh is tender and the flavors are well blended.
7. Garnish with the chopped green onion before serving.

Spaghetti Squash with Lentil Sauce

Time: 3 hours 30 minutes
Serving Size: 2 bowls
Prep Time: 20 minutes
Cook Time: 3 hours 10 minutes

Each Serving Has:
Calories: 340, Carbohydrates: 45g, Saturated Fat: 1g, Protein: 17g, Fat: 11g, Sodium: 310mg, Potassium: 920mg, Fiber: 10g, Sugar: 7g, Vitamin C: 20mg, Calcium: 70mg, Iron: 4.3mg

Ingredients:
- 1 small spaghetti squash (about 2 1/2 cups [475g] cooked strands)
- 3/4 cup [144g] cooked green lentils
- 1/2 cup [120ml] canned crushed tomatoes (low-sodium)
- 1/4 cup [40g] chopped yellow onion
- 1 clove garlic, minced
- 1 tbsp tomato paste (no salt added)
- 1/2 cup [120ml] low-sodium vegetable broth
- 1 tbsp olive oil
- 1/2 tsp dried oregano
- 1/2 tsp dried basil
- 1/4 tsp sea salt
- 1/4 tsp black pepper
- 1 tbsp chopped fresh parsley

Directions:
1. Cut the spaghetti squash in half, remove the seeds, and place the squash, cut side down, in the slow cooker.
2. Add the cooked lentils, crushed tomatoes, chopped onion, and minced garlic around the squash.
3. Stir in the tomato paste, oregano, basil, sea salt, and black pepper.
4. Pour in the vegetable broth and drizzle the olive oil over everything.
5. Stir gently to mix the sauce ingredients.
6. Cover and cook on low for 3 hours and 10 minutes, until the squash is tender.
7. Shred the squash with a fork and toss it with the sauce mixture.
8. Garnish with the chopped fresh parsley before serving.

Vegan Moroccan Tagine

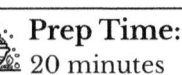

⏱ Time: 3 hours 30 minutes	🍴 Serving Size: 2 bowls
🍚 Prep Time: 20 minutes	🍲 Cook Time: 3 hours 10 minutes

Each Serving Has:
Calories: 345, Carbohydrates: 52g, Saturated Fat: 1g, Protein: 12g, Fat: 10g, Sodium: 300mg, Potassium: 940mg, Fiber: 11g, Sugar: 8g, Vitamin C: 24mg, Calcium: 75mg, Iron: 4.5mg

Ingredients:
- 3/4 cup [144g] cooked chickpeas
- 1/2 cup [80g] cubed butternut squash
- 1/2 cup [80g] chopped carrots
- 1/4 cup [40g] chopped red onion
- 1/4 cup [40g] chopped tomatoes
- 2 tbsp raisins
- 1 clove garlic, minced
- 1/2 tsp ground cumin
- 1/2 tsp ground cinnamon
- 1/4 tsp ground turmeric
- 1/4 tsp sea salt
- 1 tbsp olive oil
- 1/2 cup [120ml] low-sodium vegetable broth
- 1 tbsp chopped fresh cilantro

Directions:
1. Add the cooked chickpeas, cubed butternut squash, chopped carrots, onion, tomatoes, and raisins to the slow cooker.
2. Stir in the minced garlic, cumin, cinnamon, turmeric, and sea salt.
3. Pour in the vegetable broth and drizzle the olive oil over the mixture.
4. Mix well until the spices are evenly distributed.
5. Cover and cook on low for 3 hours and 10 minutes, until the vegetables are tender and the flavors have melded together.
6. Stir gently and garnish with the chopped fresh cilantro before serving.

Maple BBQ Seitan Medallions

⏱ Time: 3 hours 30 minutes	🍴 Serving Size: 2 servings
🍚 Prep Time: 20 minutes	🍲 Cook Time: 3 hours 10 minutes

Each Serving Has:
Calories: 360, Carbohydrates: 32g, Saturated Fat: 1g, Protein: 26g, Fat: 12g, Sodium: 420mg, Potassium: 580mg, Fiber: 4g, Sugar: 10g, Vitamin C: 5mg, Calcium: 60mg, Iron: 5.1mg

Ingredients:
- 6 oz [170g] seitan, sliced into medallions
- 1/4 cup [60ml] low-sodium vegetable broth
- 1/4 cup [60ml] low-sodium tomato sauce
- 2 tbsp maple syrup
- 1 tbsp apple cider vinegar
- 1 tbsp olive oil
- 1 tbsp minced onion
- 1 clove garlic, minced
- 1/2 tsp smoked paprika
- 1/4 tsp black pepper
- 1/4 tsp sea salt
- 1/2 tsp mustard powder
- 1 tbsp chopped fresh chives

Directions:
1. Place the seitan medallions in the slow cooker in a single layer.
2. In a bowl, mix the tomato sauce, maple syrup, apple cider vinegar, vegetable broth, olive oil, minced onion, garlic, smoked paprika, black pepper, sea salt, and mustard.
3. Pour the sauce mixture evenly over the seitan.
4. Stir gently to ensure the seitan is fully coated with the sauce.
5. Cover and cook on low for 3 hours and 10 minutes, flipping the seitan medallions halfway through the cooking time.
6. Garnish with the chopped fresh chives before serving.

CHAPTER 10: PURELY PLANT-BASED

Italian Vegan Stuffed Peppers

| Time: 3 hours 30 minutes | Serving Size: 2 stuffed peppers |
| Prep Time: 20 minutes | Cook Time: 3 hours 10 minutes |

Each Serving Has:
Calories: 345, Carbohydrates: 46g, Saturated Fat: 1g, Protein: 14g, Fat: 11g, Sodium: 310mg, Potassium: 890mg, Fiber: 9g, Sugar: 8g, Vitamin C: 85mg, Calcium: 70mg, Iron: 4.2mg

Ingredients:
- 2 large red bell peppers, tops removed and seeds discarded
- 1/2 cup [95g] cooked quinoa
- 1/2 cup [130g] canned lentils, drained and rinsed
- 1/4 cup [40g] chopped zucchini
- 1/4 cup [40g] chopped cherry tomatoes
- 1/4 cup [60ml] low-sodium tomato sauce
- 1 clove garlic, minced
- 1/2 tsp dried oregano
- 1/4 tsp dried basil
- 1/4 tsp sea salt
- 1/4 tsp black pepper
- 1 tbsp olive oil
- 1 tbsp chopped fresh parsley

Directions:
1. In a bowl, combine the cooked quinoa, rinsed lentils, chopped zucchini, cherry tomatoes, minced garlic, and tomato sauce.
2. Add the oregano, basil, sea salt, black pepper, and olive oil to the mixture.
3. Stir thoroughly until all ingredients are well mixed.
4. Stuff the bell peppers tightly with the quinoa mixture.
5. Place the stuffed peppers upright in the slow cooker.
6. Cover and cook on low for 3 hours and 10 minutes, until the peppers are tender.
7. Garnish with the chopped fresh parsley before serving.

Zesty Lentil Taco Filling

| Time: 3 hours 20 minutes | Serving Size: 2 tacos |
| Prep Time: 20 minutes | Cook Time: 3 hours |

Each Serving Has:
Calories: 330, Carbohydrates: 44g, Saturated Fat: 1g, Protein: 17g, Fat: 10g, Sodium: 340mg, Potassium: 790mg, Fiber: 9g, Sugar: 5g, Vitamin C: 10mg, Calcium: 60mg, Iron: 4.5mg

Ingredients:
- 3/4 cup [144g] cooked brown lentils
- 1/4 cup [40g] chopped red onion
- 1/2 cup [80g] chopped red bell pepper
- 1/4 cup [60ml] low-sodium tomato sauce
- 1 clove garlic, minced
- 1 tbsp lime juice
- 1/2 tsp ground cumin
- 1/2 tsp smoked paprika
- 1/4 tsp chili powder
- 1/4 tsp sea salt
- 1/4 tsp black pepper
- 1 tbsp olive oil
- 1/2 cup [120ml] low-sodium vegetable broth
- 1 tbsp chopped fresh cilantro

Directions:
1. Add the cooked lentils, chopped onion, bell pepper, and minced garlic to the slow cooker.
2. Stir in the tomato sauce, lime juice, cumin, smoked paprika, chili powder, sea salt, and black pepper.
3. Pour in the vegetable broth and drizzle the olive oil over the mixture.
4. Stir well until all ingredients are evenly mixed.
5. Cover and cook on low for 3 hours, until the vegetables are tender and the flavors are well blended.
6. Stir gently and garnish with the chopped fresh cilantro before serving.

Cashew Cream Enchiladas

⏱ **Time:** 3 hours 30 minutes	🍽 **Serving Size:** 2 servings
🥣 **Prep Time:** 20 minutes	🍲 **Cook Time:** 3 hours 10 minutes

Each Serving Has:
Calories: 395, Carbohydrates: 42g, Saturated Fat: 3g, Protein: 14g, Fat: 18g, Sodium: 360mg, Potassium: 790mg, Fiber: 8g, Sugar: 6g, Vitamin C: 16mg, Calcium: 70mg, Iron: 4.4mg

Ingredients:
- 2 whole wheat tortillas
- 1/2 cup [90g] cooked black beans
- 1/2 cup [80g] chopped spinach
- 1/4 cup [40g] chopped red bell pepper
- 1/4 cup [60ml] low-sodium enchilada sauce
- 1/4 cup [35g] raw cashews, soaked
- 1/4 cup [60ml] unsweetened almond milk
- 1 clove garlic, minced
- 1 tbsp lemon juice
- 1 tbsp nutritional yeast
- 1 tbsp olive oil
- 1/4 tsp sea salt
- 1/4 tsp ground cumin
- 1 tbsp chopped fresh cilantro

Directions:
1. In a blender, combine the soaked cashews, almond milk, lemon juice, minced garlic, nutritional yeast, olive oil, cumin, and sea salt.
2. Blend until smooth and creamy to make the cashew sauce.
3. In a bowl, mix the cooked black beans, chopped spinach, and bell pepper.
4. FillEach tortilla with the mixture and roll it tightly.
5. Place the rolled tortillas seam-side down in the slow cooker.
6. Pour the enchilada sauce over the tortillas and drizzle with the cashew cream.
7. Cover and cook on low for 3 hours and 10 minutes, until heated through.
8. Garnish with the chopped fresh cilantro before serving.

Vegan Stuffed Eggplant Boats

⏱ **Time:** 3 hours 30 minutes	🍽 **Serving Size:** 2 boats
🥣 **Prep Time:** 20 minutes	🍲 **Cook Time:** 3 hours 10 minutes

Each Serving Has:
Calories: 355, Carbohydrates: 42g, Saturated Fat: 1g, Protein: 13g, Fat: 14g, Sodium: 320mg, Potassium: 880mg, Fiber: 10g, Sugar: 7g, Vitamin C: 18mg, Calcium: 65mg, Iron: 4.1mg

Ingredients:
- 1 medium eggplant, halved lengthwise and flesh scooped out
- 1/2 cup [95g] cooked quinoa
- 1/2 cup [130g] canned chickpeas, drained and rinsed
- 1/4 cup [40g] chopped cherry tomatoes
- 1/4 cup [40g] chopped red onion
- 1 clove garlic, minced
- 1/4 cup [60ml] low-sodium vegetable broth
- 1 tbsp olive oil
- 1/2 tsp dried oregano
- 1/4 tsp sea salt
- 1/4 tsp black pepper
- 1 tbsp lemon juice
- 1 tbsp chopped fresh parsley

Directions:
1. Place the hollowed eggplant halves in the slow cooker, cut side up.
2. In a bowl, mix the cooked quinoa, rinsed chickpeas, chopped cherry tomatoes, onion, and minced garlic.
3. Stir in the oregano, sea salt, black pepper, olive oil, lemon juice, and vegetable broth.
4. FillEach eggplant half with the quinoa mixture, gently pressing the filling to keep it compact.
5. Cover and cook on low for 3 hours and 10 minutes, until the eggplant is tender.
6. Garnish with the chopped fresh parsley before serving.

CHAPTER 10: PURELY PLANT-BASED

Miso Glazed Sweet Potatoes

🕒 **Time:** 3 hours 30 minutes	🍽 **Serving Size:** 2 plates
🍚 **Prep Time:** 20 minutes	🍲 **Cook Time:** 3 hours 10 minutes

Each Serving Has:
Calories: 320, Carbohydrates: 45g, Saturated Fat: 1g, Protein: 7g, Fat: 12g, Sodium: 370mg, Potassium: 780mg, Fiber: 6g, Sugar: 11g, Vitamin C: 22mg, Calcium: 55mg, Iron: 2.3mg

Ingredients:
- 2 medium sweet potatoes, peeled and cubed (about 2 cups [260g])
- 1/4 cup [60ml] low-sodium vegetable broth
- 1 tbsp white miso paste
- 1 tbsp maple syrup
- 1 tbsp rice vinegar
- 1 tbsp olive oil
- 1 tbsp low-sodium soy sauce
- 1 clove garlic, minced
- 1/2 tsp grated fresh ginger
- 1/4 tsp black pepper
- 1 tbsp chopped green onion

Directions:
1. Place the cubed sweet potatoes at the bottom of the slow cooker.
2. In a small bowl, whisk together the white miso paste, maple syrup, rice vinegar, olive oil, and soy sauce.
3. Pour in the vegetable broth and stir thoroughly.
4. Add the minced garlic, grated ginger, and black pepper to the bowl.
5. Stir the glaze mixture until thoroughly combined.
6. Pour the glaze over the sweet potatoes in the slow cooker.
7. Mix well to coat all the pieces evenly.
8. Cover and cook on low for 3 hours and 10 minutes, until the sweet potatoes are tender.
9. Garnish with the chopped green onion before serving.

Spiced Tofu Veggie Loaf

🕒 **Time:** 3 hours 30 minutes	🍽 **Serving Size:** 2 slices
🍚 **Prep Time:** 20 minutes	🍲 **Cook Time:** 3 hours 10 minutes

Each Serving Has:
Calories: 340, Carbohydrates: 28g, Saturated Fat: 1g, Protein: 19g, Fat: 15g, Sodium: 350mg, Potassium: 720mg, Fiber: 6g, Sugar: 5g, Vitamin C: 16mg, Calcium: 140mg, Iron: 4.8mg

Ingredients:
- 8 oz [227g] extra-firm tofu, pressed and crumbled
- 1/4 cup [40g] grated carrot
- 1/4 cup [40g] finely chopped celery
- 1/4 cup [40g] finely chopped onion
- 2 tbsp rolled oats
- 1 tbsp ground flaxseed
- 1 tbsp tomato paste (no salt added)
- 1 tbsp olive oil
- 1 tbsp low-sodium soy sauce
- 1 clove garlic, minced
- 1/2 tsp smoked paprika
- 1/4 tsp ground cumin
- 1/4 tsp sea salt
- 1/4 tsp black pepper

Directions:
1. In a bowl, combine the crumbled tofu, rolled oats, ground flaxseed, tomato paste, soy sauce, and olive oil.
2. Stir in the grated carrot, chopped celery, onion, minced garlic, smoked paprika, cumin, sea salt, and black pepper.
3. Mix well until the ingredients stick together.
4. Form the mixture into a compact loaf shape.
5. Place the loaf into the slow cooker lined with parchment paper.
6. Cover and cook on low for 3 hours and 10 minutes, until the loaf is firm and cooked through.
7. Let the loaf cool for 10 minutes before slicing.

Slow Cooker Vegan "Meatballs"

Time: 3 hours 30 minutes
Serving Size: 2 servings
Prep Time: 20 minutes
Cook Time: 3 hours 10 minutes

Each Serving Has:
Calories: 370, Carbohydrates: 30g, Saturated Fat: 1g, Protein: 20g, Fat: 17g, Sodium: 360mg, Potassium: 740mg, Fiber: 7g, Sugar: 5g, Vitamin C: 10mg, Calcium: 90mg, Iron: 4.9mg

Ingredients:
- 3/4 cup [130g] cooked lentils, mashed
- 1/4 cup [40g] finely chopped mushrooms
- 1/4 cup [40g] finely chopped onion
- 2 tbsp rolled oats
- 1 tbsp ground flaxseed
- 1 tbsp tomato paste (no salt added)
- 1 tbsp low-sodium soy sauce
- 1 tbsp olive oil
- 1 clove garlic, minced
- 1/2 tsp dried oregano
- 1/4 tsp black pepper
- 1/4 tsp sea salt
- 1/2 cup [120ml] low-sodium marinara sauce
- 1 tbsp chopped fresh basil

Directions:
1. In a bowl, combine the mashed lentils, chopped mushrooms, onion, rolled oats, ground flaxseed, tomato paste, and soy sauce.
2. Add the olive oil, minced garlic, oregano, sea salt, and black pepper to the mixture.
3. Stir until everything is thoroughly combined and firm enough to shape.
4. Roll the mixture into small, compact balls.
5. Place the «meatballs» into the slow cooker.
6. Pour the marinara sauce evenly over the top of the meatballs.
7. Cover and cook on low for 3 hours and 10 minutes, until the meatballs are cooked through.
8. Garnish with the chopped fresh basil before serving.

Vegan Chickpea Bake with Avocado

Time: 3 hours 30 minutes
Serving Size: 2 servings
Prep Time: 20 minutes
Cook Time: 3 hours 10 minutes

Each Serving Has:
Calories: 395, Carbohydrates: 36g, Saturated Fat: 2g, Protein: 14g, Fat: 20g, Sodium: 340mg, Potassium: 870mg, Fiber: 10g, Sugar: 5g, Vitamin C: 18mg, Calcium: 70mg, Iron: 4.6mg

Ingredients:
- 3/4 cup [130g] cooked chickpeas
- 1/4 cup [40g] chopped red bell pepper
- 1/4 cup [40g] chopped zucchini
- 1/4 cup [40g] chopped red onion
- 1/4 cup [60ml] unsweetened almond milk
- 1 tbsp olive oil
- 1 tbsp nutritional yeast
- 1 tbsp lemon juice
- 1/2 tsp garlic powder
- 1/2 tsp smoked paprika
- 1/4 tsp sea salt
- 1/4 tsp black pepper
- 1/2 medium avocado, sliced
- 1 tbsp chopped fresh cilantro

Directions:
1. Add the cooked chickpeas, chopped bell pepper, zucchini, and onion to the slow cooker.
2. In a bowl, mix the almond milk, olive oil, nutritional yeast, lemon juice, garlic powder, smoked paprika, sea salt, and black pepper.
3. Stir the liquid mixture until smooth and well combined.
4. Pour the sauce over the vegetables and chickpeas in the slow cooker.
5. Stir gently to distribute the sauce evenly.
6. Cover and cook on low for 3 hours and 10 minutes, until the vegetables are tender.
7. Top with the sliced avocado and garnish with the chopped fresh cilantro before serving.

CHAPTER 10: PURELY PLANT-BASED

Cabbage & Avocado Wrap

Time: 3 hours 20 minutes
Serving Size: 2 wraps
Prep Time: 20 minutes
Cook Time: 3 hours

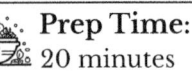

Each Serving Has:
Calories: 360, Carbohydrates: 32g, Saturated Fat: 2g, Protein: 10g, Fat: 22g, Sodium: 310mg, Potassium: 870mg, Fiber: 9g, Sugar: 6g, Vitamin C: 35mg, Calcium: 60mg, Iron: 3.5mg

Ingredients:
- 2 large cabbage leaves, trimmed for wrapping
- 3/4 cup [130g] cooked chickpeas
- 1/4 cup [40g] shredded carrots
- 1/4 cup [40g] chopped red bell pepper
- 2 tbsp finely chopped red onion
- 1/4 cup [60ml] unsweetened almond milk
- 1 tbsp olive oil
- 1 tbsp tahini
- 1 tbsp lemon juice
- 1 clove garlic, minced
- 1/4 tsp ground cumin
- 1/4 tsp sea salt
- 1/4 tsp black pepper
- 1/2 medium avocado, sliced
- 1 tbsp chopped fresh parsley

Directions:
1. Add the cooked chickpeas, shredded carrots, chopped bell pepper, and onion to the slow cooker.
2. In a bowl, mix the almond milk, olive oil, tahini, lemon juice, minced garlic, cumin, sea salt, and black pepper.
3. Stir the dressing mixture until smooth and well combined.
4. Pour the dressing over the vegetables and chickpeas in the slow cooker.
5. Mix gently to combine all ingredients.
6. Cover and cook on low for 3 hours, until the vegetables are tender.
7. Spoon the filling into the cabbage leaves, and top with sliced avocado.
8. Garnish with the chopped fresh parsley before serving.

Lemon Garlic Tempeh Strips

Time: 3 hours 20 minutes
Serving Size: 2 servings
Prep Time: 20 minutes
Cook Time: 3 hours

Each Serving Has:
Calories: 360, Carbohydrates: 16g, Saturated Fat: 2g, Protein: 20g, Fat: 22g, Sodium: 330mg, Potassium: 690mg, Fiber: 4g, Sugar: 4g, Vitamin C: 14mg, Calcium: 90mg, Iron: 3.2mg

Ingredients:
- 8 oz [227g] tempeh, sliced into strips
- 1 tbsp olive oil
- 2 tbsp lemon juice
- 1 clove garlic, minced
- 1/4 cup [60ml] low-sodium vegetable broth
- 1/2 tsp dried thyme
- 1/4 tsp black pepper
- 1/4 tsp sea salt
- 1/4 tsp smoked paprika
- 1/2 lemon, sliced into rounds
- 1 tbsp chopped parsley

Directions:
1. Place the tempeh strips in the base of the slow cooker.
2. In a small bowl, mix the olive oil, lemon juice, minced garlic, vegetable broth, thyme, black pepper, sea salt, and smoked paprika.
3. Stir well to combine into a marinade.
4. Pour the marinade evenly over the tempeh strips.
5. Add the lemon slices on top of the tempeh.
6. Cover and cook on low for 3 hours, until the tempeh is tender and flavorful.
7. Let cool slightly and garnish with the chopped fresh parsley before serving.

Chapter 11: Sweet Comforts

Choco-Chia Pudding Cake

Time: 3 hours 20 minutes	Serving Size: 2 servings
Prep Time: 20 minutes	Cook Time: 3 hours

Each Serving Has:
Calories: 310, Carbohydrates: 36g, Saturated Fat: 3g, Protein: 8g, Fat: 15g, Sodium: 120mg, Potassium: 430mg, Fiber: 9g, Sugar: 16g, Vitamin C: 0mg, Calcium: 140mg, Iron: 3.2mg

Ingredients:
- 1/4 cup [60ml] unsweetened almond milk
- 1/4 cup [60g] unsweetened applesauce
- 1/4 cup [60ml] light coconut milk (plus extra for greasing)
- 2 tbsp maple syrup
- 2 tbsp chia seeds
- 2 tbsp unsweetened cocoa powder
- 2 tbsp rolled oats
- 1/4 tsp vanilla extract
- 1/8 tsp ground cinnamon
- 1/8 tsp sea salt
- 1 tbsp chopped dark chocolate (70% or higher)
- 1 tbsp crushed walnuts

Directions:
1. In a bowl, whisk together the almond milk, applesauce, light coconut milk, maple syrup, and vanilla extract.
2. Stir in the chia seeds, cocoa powder, rolled oats, cinnamon, and sea salt.
3. Mix well until the cocoa is fully dissolved and the chia seeds are evenly distributed.
4. Lightly grease the bottom of the slow cooker with a drop of coconut milk.
5. Pour the mixture evenly into the slow cooker.
6. Sprinkle the chopped dark chocolate on top of the batter.
7. Cover and cook on low for 3 hours, until the mixture is set and the flavors have melded.
8. Garnish with the crushed walnuts before serving.

Maple Pecan Sticky Rice

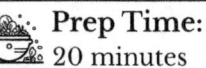

⏰ Time: 3 hours 20 minutes	🍽 Serving Size: 2 bowls
🍲 Prep Time: 20 minutes	🍳 Cook Time: 3 hours

Each Serving Has:
Calories: 385, Carbohydrates: 52g, Saturated Fat: 3g, Protein: 6g, Fat: 17g, Sodium: 85mg, Potassium: 220mg, Fiber: 3g, Sugar: 18g, Vitamin C: 0mg, Calcium: 50mg, Iron: 2mg

Ingredients:
- 1/2 cup [100g] short-grain white rice
- 3/4 cup [180ml] light coconut milk
- 2 tbsp maple syrup
- 1 tbsp brown rice syrup
- 1 tbsp chopped pecans (plus 1 tbsp for garnish)
- 1/2 tsp vanilla extract
- 1/4 tsp ground cinnamon
- 1/8 tsp sea salt
- 2 tbsp water
- 1 tsp maple syrup

Directions:
1. Rinse the short-grain white rice under cold water until the water runs clear.
2. Add the rinsed rice, light coconut milk, maple syrup, brown rice syrup, and water to the slow cooker.
3. Stir in the chopped pecans, vanilla extract, cinnamon, and sea salt.
4. Mix well to distribute all ingredients evenly.
5. Cover and cook on low for 3 hours, stirring once halfway through the cooking time.
6. Let cool slightly. Garnish with additional chopped pecans and drizzle with maple syrup before serving.

Spiced Apple Cobbler

⏰ Time: 3 hours 20 minutes	🍽 Serving Size: 2 bowls
🍲 Prep Time: 20 minutes	🍳 Cook Time: 3 hours

Each Serving Has:
Calories: 340, Carbohydrates: 50g, Saturated Fat: 2g, Protein: 4g, Fat: 12g, Sodium: 95mg, Potassium: 270mg, Fiber: 5g, Sugar: 27g, Vitamin C: 8mg, Calcium: 60mg, Iron: 1.8mg

Ingredients:
- 2 medium apples, peeled and sliced
- 2 tbsp maple syrup
- 1 tbsp lemon juice
- 1/2 tsp ground cinnamon
- 1/8 tsp ground nutmeg
- 1/4 cup [30g] whole wheat flour
- 2 tbsp rolled oats
- 1 tbsp almond flour
- 2 tbsp coconut oil, solid
- 1 tbsp unsweetened almond milk
- 1/8 tsp sea salt
- 1 tbsp chopped walnuts

Directions:
1. In a bowl, toss the sliced apples with lemon juice, maple syrup, cinnamon, and nutmeg.
2. Place the apple mixture in the base of the slow cooker.
3. In another bowl, mix the whole wheat flour, rolled oats, almond flour, and sea salt.
4. Cut in the coconut oil until the mixture becomes crumbly.
5. Add the almond milk and mix to form a rough dough.
6. Spoon the dough evenly over the apples and press gently.
7. Cover and cook on low for 3 hours, until the apples are tender and the topping is golden.
8. Top with the chopped walnuts before serving.

Slow-Cooked Choco Banana Bread

⏱ **Time:** 3 hours 15 minutes	🍴 **Serving Size:** 2 servings
🥣 **Prep Time:** 15 minutes	🍲 **Cook Time:** 3 hours

Each Serving Has:
Calories: 360, Carbohydrates: 52g, Saturated Fat: 3g, Protein: 6g, Fat: 14g, Sodium: 160mg, Potassium: 310mg, Fiber: 5g, Sugar: 24g, Vitamin C: 6mg, Calcium: 45mg, Iron: 2.2mg

Ingredients:
- 1 large ripe banana, mashed
- 1/4 cup [60ml] unsweetened almond milk
- 2 tbsp maple syrup
- 1/2 tsp vanilla extract
- 1/2 cup [60g] whole wheat flour
- 2 tbsp almond flour
- 2 tbsp unsweetened cocoa powder
- 1/2 tsp baking powder
- 1/8 tsp baking soda
- 1/8 tsp sea salt
- 1 tbsp dark chocolate chips
- 1 tbsp chopped walnuts (optional)

Directions:
1. In a bowl, mash the ripe banana until smooth.
2. Add the unsweetened almond milk, maple syrup, and vanilla extract, then stir until combined.
3. In another bowl, mix the whole wheat flour, almond flour, cocoa powder, baking powder, baking soda, and sea salt.
4. Combine the wet and dry mixtures until just blended.
5. Fold in the dark chocolate chips and chopped walnuts (if using).
6. Line the base of a small slow cooker with parchment paper.
7. Pour the batter into the slow cooker and smooth the top.
8. Cover and cook on low for 3 hours, until a toothpick inserted comes out clean.
9. Let the bread cool for 10 minutes before slicing.

Almond Butter Fudge Brownies

⏱ **Time:** 3 hours 20 minutes	🍴 **Serving Size:** 2 servings
🥣 **Prep Time:** 20 minutes	🍲 **Cook Time:** 3 hours

Each Serving Has:
Calories: 385, Carbohydrates: 30g, Saturated Fat: 3g, Protein: 8g, Fat: 25g, Sodium: 125mg, Potassium: 280mg, Fiber: 6g, Sugar: 14g, Vitamin C: 0mg, Calcium: 58mg, Iron: 2.1mg

Ingredients:
- 1/3 cup [80ml] unsweetened almond milk
- 1/4 cup [64g] almond butter
- 2 tbsp maple syrup
- 1 tsp vanilla extract
- 1/2 cup [60g] almond flour
- 2 tbsp unsweetened cocoa powder
- 2 tbsp oat flour
- 1/2 tsp baking powder
- 1/8 tsp sea salt
- 2 tbsp dark chocolate chips

Directions:
1. In a mixing bowl, combine the almond milk, almond butter, maple syrup, and vanilla extract.
2. In a separate bowl, mix the almond flour, cocoa powder, oat flour, baking powder, and sea salt.
3. Stir the wet mixture into the dry ingredients until fully combined.
4. Fold in the dark chocolate chips gently.
5. Lightly grease a small baking insert or line it with parchment paper.
6. Pour the batter into the insert and spread it evenly.
7. Place the insert in the slow cooker and cover.
8. Cook on low until firm, about 3 hours, or until a toothpick inserted comes out clean.
9. Let the fudge cool for 10 minutes before slicing.

CHAPTER 11: SWEET COMFORTS

Coconut Vanilla Rice Pudding

Time: 3 hours 10 minutes	Serving Size: 2 bowls
Prep Time: 10 minutes	Cook Time: 3 hours

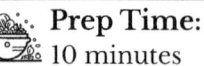

Each Serving Has:
Calories: 345, Carbohydrates: 50g, Saturated Fat: 10g, Protein: 5g, Fat: 14g, Sodium: 45mg, Potassium: 180mg, Fiber: 2g, Sugar: 11g, Vitamin C: 1mg, Calcium: 36mg, Iron: 2mg

Ingredients:
- 1/2 cup [96g] short-grain white rice
- 1 cup [240ml] canned light coconut milk
- 1/2 cup [120ml] water
- 2 tbsp maple syrup
- 1/2 tsp vanilla extract
- 1/8 tsp ground cinnamon
- 1/8 tsp sea salt
- 1/2 tbsp chia seeds
- 1 tbsp unsweetened shredded coconut

Directions:
1. Rinse the short-grain white rice under cold water until the water runs clear.
2. In a slow cooker, combine the rinsed rice, coconut milk, water, maple syrup, and vanilla extract.
3. Add the cinnamon, sea salt, and chia seeds, stirring well to incorporate.
4. Cover the slow cooker with the lid and cook on low for 3 hours.
5. Stir the mixture gently once every hour during cooking to prevent sticking and ensure even consistency.
6. When the rice is thick and creamy, stir in the shredded coconut.
7. Let the pudding rest for a few minutes before serving.

Orange Cranberry Bread Pudding

Time: 3 hours 15 minutes	Serving Size: 2 bowls
Prep Time: 15 minutes	Cook Time: 3 hours

Each Serving Has:
Calories: 310, Carbohydrates: 48g, Saturated Fat: 5g, Protein: 6g, Fat: 10g, Sodium: 120mg, Potassium: 210mg, Fiber: 4g, Sugar: 19g, Vitamin C: 9mg, Calcium: 75mg, Iron: 2mg

Ingredients:
- 2 cups [140g] cubed whole grain plant-based bread
- 1/2 cup [120ml] unsweetened almond milk
- 1/4 cup [60ml] canned light coconut milk
- 1/4 cup [30g] dried cranberries
- 1 tbsp maple syrup
- 1 tbsp orange juice
- 1 tsp orange zest
- 1/2 tsp vanilla extract
- 1/4 tsp ground cinnamon
- 1/8 tsp sea salt
- 1 tsp coconut oil (optional)

Directions:
1. Lightly grease the inside of the slow cooker with a small amount of coconut oil or use parchment paper.
2. In a large bowl, combine the almond milk, light coconut milk, maple syrup, orange juice, orange zest, vanilla extract, cinnamon, and sea salt.
3. Stir well to blend all the wet ingredients evenly.
4. Add the cubed bread and dried cranberries to the bowl and toss to coat the bread with the liquid mixture.
5. Let the mixture sit for 10 minutes so the bread absorbs the liquid.
6. Pour everything into the slow cooker and spread it out evenly.
7. Cover and cook on low heat for 3 hours, until the top is golden and the edges are set.
8. Let the pudding cool slightly before serving.

Carrot Cake Oat Bars

Time: 3 hours 10 minutes
Serving Size: 2 bars
Prep Time: 10 minutes
Cook Time: 3 hours

Each Serving Has:
Calories: 285, Carbohydrates: 42g, Saturated Fat: 3g, Protein: 6g, Fat: 9g, Sodium: 115mg, Potassium: 320mg, Fiber: 5g, Sugar: 15g, Vitamin C: 2mg, Calcium: 80mg, Iron: 2mg

Ingredients:
- 1 cup [90g] rolled oats
- 1/2 cup [60g] grated carrots
- 1/4 cup [60ml] unsweetened almond milk
- 1/4 cup [60ml] maple syrup
- 1/4 cup [28g] chopped walnuts
- 1 tbsp unsweetened shredded coconut
- 1 tbsp ground flaxseed
- 1 tsp vanilla extract
- 1/2 tsp ground cinnamon
- 1/4 tsp ground nutmeg
- 1/8 tsp sea salt
- 1 tsp coconut oil (optional)

Directions:
1. Lightly grease the slow cooker with a small amount of coconut oil or line it with parchment paper to prevent sticking.
2. In a mixing bowl, combine the almond milk, maple syrup, vanilla extract, and ground flaxseed. Let the mixture sit for 5 minutes to thicken slightly.
3. Add the rolled oats, grated carrots, chopped walnuts, shredded coconut, cinnamon, nutmeg, and sea salt to the bowl.
4. Stir until all ingredients are well mixed and the oats are evenly coated.
5. Pour the mixture into the prepared slow cooker and spread it into an even layer.
6. Cover and cook on low for 3 hours, or until the bars are firm and lightly browned at the edges.
7. Turn off the heat, let cool in the slow cooker for 10–15 minutes, then remove and slice into bars.

Vegan Chocolate Lava Pots

Time: 2 hours 20 minutes
Serving Size: 2 servings
Prep Time: 20 minutes
Cook Time: 2 hours

Each Serving Has:
Calories: 310, Carbohydrates: 40g, Saturated Fat: 3g, Protein: 5g, Fat: 14g, Sodium: 85mg, Potassium: 290mg, Fiber: 5g, Sugar: 24g, Vitamin C: 0mg, Calcium: 35mg, Iron: 3.2mg

Ingredients:
- 1/2 cup [120ml] unsweetened almond milk
- 1/4 cup [30g] whole wheat flour
- 1/4 cup [30g] unsweetened cocoa powder
- 1/4 cup [60ml] maple syrup
- 2 tbsp melted coconut oil (plus extra for greasing)
- 1 oz [28g] dark vegan chocolate, chopped
- 1/2 tsp baking powder
- 1/4 tsp vanilla extract
- 1/8 tsp sea salt

Directions:
1. Lightly grease two heat-safe ramekins with coconut oil.
2. In a bowl, whisk together the almond milk, maple syrup, vanilla extract, and melted coconut oil.
3. Sift in the cocoa powder, whole wheat flour, baking powder, and sea salt.
4. Stir until smooth and well combined.
5. Pour the batter evenly into the prepared ramekins.
6. Place half of the chopped dark vegan chocolate in the center ofEach ramekin.
7. Cover the ramekins with foil and place them in the slow cooker.
8. Cook on low for 2 hours, until the cakes are set and a toothpick comes out clean.
9. Let the cakes cool for 10 minutes before serving.

CHAPTER 11: SWEET COMFORTS

Warm Blueberry Crumble

Time: 3 hours 15 minutes
Serving Size: 2 bowls
Prep Time: 15 minutes
Cook Time: 3 hours

Each Serving Has:
Calories: 310, Carbohydrates: 48g, Saturated Fat: 3g, Protein: 5g, Fat: 12g, Sodium: 105mg, Potassium: 290mg, Fiber: 6g, Sugar: 21g, Vitamin C: 12mg, Calcium: 60mg, Iron: 2mg

Ingredients:
- 1 1/2 cups [225g] fresh blueberries
- 1/2 cup [45g] rolled oats
- 1/4 cup [30g] almond flour
- 2 tbsp chopped pecans
- 2 tbsp maple syrup
- 1 tbsp coconut oil, melted (plus extra for greasing, optional)
- 1 tbsp ground flaxseed
- 1/2 tsp ground cinnamon
- 1/2 tsp vanilla extract
- 1/8 tsp sea salt

Directions:
1. Lightly grease the bottom of the slow cooker with a small amount of coconut oil or line with parchment paper.
2. In a bowl, toss the fresh blueberries with the vanilla extract and transfer them to the slow cooker.
3. In a separate bowl, mix the rolled oats, almond flour, chopped pecans, ground flaxseed, cinnamon, and sea salt.
4. Drizzle the maple syrup and melted coconut oil into the oat mixture and stir until combined.
5. Sprinkle the crumble mixture evenly over the blueberries in the slow cooker.
6. Cover and cook on low for 3 hours, until the top is golden and the berries are bubbling.
7. Let the crumble sit for 10–15 minutes before serving to thicken slightly.

Cinnamon Pear Compote

Time: 3 hours 10 minutes
Serving Size: 2 bowls
Prep Time: 10 minutes
Cook Time: 3 hours

Each Serving Has:
Calories: 195, Carbohydrates: 44g, Saturated Fat: 0g, Protein: 1g, Fat: 1g, Sodium: 2mg, Potassium: 220mg, Fiber: 5g, Sugar: 29g, Vitamin C: 10mg, Calcium: 20mg, Iron: 0.6mg

Ingredients:
- 3 ripe pears, peeled and diced
- 1/4 cup [60ml] orange juice
- 2 tbsp maple syrup
- 1 tbsp raisins
- 1/2 tsp ground cinnamon
- 1/4 tsp ground ginger
- 1/4 tsp vanilla extract
- 1/16 tsp ground cloves

Directions:
1. Add the diced pears to the bottom of the slow cooker.
2. Pour in the orange juice and maple syrup.
3. Stir in the raisins, cinnamon, ginger, and cloves.
4. Drizzle the vanilla extract over the mixture.
5. Cover and cook on low for 3 hours, until the pears are tender and the mixture has thickened.
6. Stir gently to combine and let the compote cool for a few minutes before serving.

Chapter 12: 28-Day Meal Prep Plan

Week	Day	Breakfast	Lunch	Snack or appetizer	Dinner
Week 1:	1	Blueberry Lemon Breakfast Quinoa	Rustic Tomato Lentil Soup	Smoky Maple Chickpeas	Rustic Tofu Pot Roast
	2	Maple Chia Oatmeal Delight	Spicy Brown Rice & Mushroom Stew	Slow-Roasted Spiced Nuts	Lentil & Root Veg Shepherd's Pie
	3	Cinnamon Apple Buckwheat Bowl	Creamy Broccoli & Pea Soup	Buffalo Cauliflower Bites	Stuffed Squash with Wild Rice
	4	Golden Turmeric Oats	Moroccan Chickpea Stew	Ginger-Garlic Edamame	Tofu and Veggie Stroganoff
	5	Peanut Butter Cacao Oats	Butternut Squash Apple Soup	Slow-Cooked Salsa Dip	Mediterranean Chickpea Bake
	6	Apple Pie Cauliflower Bowl	Lemon Dill Split Pea Soup	Herb & Olive Bean Medley	Mushroom Bourguignon
	7	Warm Fig & Hazelnut Farro	Italian White Bean Stew	Sweet Potato Tot Cups	Slow-Cooked Eggplant Parmesan
Week 2:	8	Tropical Mango Quinoa Mash	Zucchini Basil Bisque	Sticky Sesame Mushrooms	Creamy Polenta with Ratatouille
	9	Sweet Potato Pie Oats	Curried Carrot Ginger Soup	Zesty Lentil Poppers	Sweet Potato and Peanut Casserole
	10	Banana Bread Breakfast Oats	Roasted Red Pepper Soup	Jalapeño Corn Dip	Balsamic Glazed Cauliflower Steaks
	11	Vanilla Pear Millet Bowl	Kale & Potato Comfort Stew	Vegan Spinach Artichoke Dip	Tamari Tempeh & Veggie Skillet
	12	Lavender Vanilla Barley Bowl	Cabbage and Fennel Soup	Cashew Carrot Spread	Portobello and Barley Bake
	13	Strawberry Basil Chia Pudding	Black Garlic Veggie Broth	Roasted Red Pepper Hummus	Vegan Jambalaya
	14	Creamy Coconut Quinoa Porridge	Sweet Potato Corn Chowder	Coconut Curry Popcorn Mix	Cheesy Vegan Cauliflower Gratin

Week	Day	Breakfast	Lunch	Snack or appetizer	Dinner
Week 3:	15	Maple Chia Oatmeal Delight	Lemon Garlic Orzo	Sticky Sesame Mushrooms	Slow Cooker Stuffed Cabbage Rolls
	16	Almond Banana Millet Mash	Thai Peanut Noodle Bowl	Zesty Lentil Poppers	Chickpea Tikka Masala
	17	Coconut Date Breakfast Rice	Thai-Inspired Coconut Soup	Jalapeño Corn Dip	Thai Red Lentil Curry
	18	Banana Bread Breakfast Oats	Spiced Tofu Veggie Loaf	Cashew Carrot Spread	Spicy Black Bean Chili
	19	Golden Turmeric Oats	Cashew Cream Enchiladas	Caramelized Onion Bruschetta	Coconut Sweet Potato Curry
	20	Blueberry Lemon Breakfast Quinoa	Pesto Pasta with White Beans	Vegan Spinach Artichoke Dip	Jamaican Jerk Veggie Stew
	21	Lavender Vanilla Barley Bowl	Zesty Lentil Taco Filling	BBQ Pulled Mushroom Sliders	Butternut Chickpea Curry
Week 4:	22	Cinnamon Apple Buckwheat Bowl	Smoky Cannellini with Spinach	Ginger-Garlic Edamame	White Bean & Kale Chili
	23	Apple Pie Cauliflower Bowl	Lemon Garlic Tempeh Strips	Herb & Olive Bean Medley	Creamy Cashew Cauliflower Curry
	24	Tropical Mango Quinoa Mash	Smoky Tempeh Chili	Sweet Potato Tot Cups	Cajun Black-Eyed Peas
	25	Sweet Potato Pie Oats	Vegan Moroccan Tagine	Slow-Roasted Spiced Nuts	Brown Rice & Pinto Bowl
	26	Warm Fig & Hazelnut Farro	Lemony Farro and Fava Beans	Slow-Cooked Salsa Dip	Savory Chickpeas with Wild Rice
	27	Strawberry Basil Chia Pudding	Barley and Vegetable Pilaf	Buffalo Cauliflower Bites	Creamy Tomato Penne Bake
	28	Creamy Coconut Quinoa Porridge	Slow Cooker Vegan "Meatballs"	Smoky Maple Chickpeas	Garlic Alfredo Zucchini Pasta

Free Gift

Thank you! Discover your gift inside! Dive into a rich assortment of DASH Diet for Beginners recipes for added inspiration. Gift it or share the PDF effortlessly with friends and family via a single click on WhatsApp or other social platforms. Bon appétit!

Conclusion outline

Embracing a plant-based slow cooker lifestyle is a powerful commitment to both personal wellness and sustainable living. Throughout this cookbook, you've discovered how hearty, flavorful, and nourishing plant-based meals can come together effortlessly with the help of a slow cooker. WithEach recipe, you've gained confidence in crafting satisfying dishes that align with your health goals while fitting seamlessly into your busy life.

What begins as a practical way to simplify mealtime often becomes something more—a shift in how we think about food and nourishment. As you've explored these recipes, you've likely noticed the benefits of a diet centered around whole, plant-based Ingredients: improved digestion, steady energy, and a lighter, more vibrant feeling overall. These meals are designed not just to fuel your body, but to support your heart, mind, and long-term health.

More than just a collection of recipes, this cookbook has offered a framework for sustainable eating—one that respects your time, your body, and the planet. By leaning on the slow cooker, you've learned to maximize flavor with minimal effort, making plant-based cooking not only achievable but truly enjoyable.Each dish is a small step toward a more conscious, compassionate way of living.

Above all, this journey is about progress, not perfection. Whether you're fully plant-based or simply adding more meatless meals into your week, every choice you make has a meaningful impact. Let your slow cooker continue to be your ally in this lifestyle, making healthy eating approachable, consistent, and delicious.

So keep experimenting, stay curious, and savor the process. Your path to vibrant health is just starting, and withEach slow-cooked meal, you're reinforcing a lifestyle that nourishes you from the inside out. Here's to many more warm, plant-powered meals ahead!

References

Barnard, N. D. (2011). 21-Day Weight Loss Kickstart: Boost Metabolism, Lower Cholesterol, and Dramatically Improve Your Health. Grand Central Life & Style.

Campbell, T. C., & Campbell, T. M. (2006). The China Study: The Most Comprehensive Study of Nutrition Ever Conducted and the Startling Implications for Diet, Weight Loss, and Long-Term Health. BenBella Books.

Fuhrman, J. (2011). Eat to Live: The Amazing Nutrient-Rich Program for Fast and Sustained Weight Loss. Little, Brown Spark.

Greger, M., & Stone, G. (2015). How Not to Die: Discover the Foods Scientifically Proven to Prevent and Reverse Disease. Flatiron Books.

McDougall, J., & McDougall, M. (2013). The Starch Solution: Eat the Foods You Love, Regain Your Health, and Lose the Weight for Good!. Rodale Books.

Esselstyn, C. B. (2007). Prevent and Reverse Heart Disease: The Revolutionary, Scientifically Proven, Nutrition-Based Cure. Avery Publishing.

Melina, V., Craig, W., & Levin, S. (2016). Position of the Academy of Nutrition and Dietetics: Vegetarian Diets. Journal of the Academy of Nutrition and Dietetics, 116(12), 1970–1980.

Leitzmann, C. (2014). Vegetarian nutrition: past, present, future. The American Journal of Clinical Nutrition, 100(Suppl_1), 496S–502S.

U.S. Department of Agriculture (USDA) & U.S. Department of Health and Human Services (HHS). (2020). Dietary Guidelines for Americans 2020–2025. Retrieved from https://www.dietaryguidelines.gov/

Harvard T.H. Chan School of Public Health. (2023). The Nutrition Source – Vegetables and Fruits. Retrieved from https://www.hsph.harvard.edu/nutritionsource/

National Institutes of Health (NIH). (2023). Plant-Based Diets and Health. Retrieved from https://www.nih.gov/

Centers for Disease Control and Prevention (CDC). (2023). Healthy Eating for a Healthy Heart. Retrieved from https://www.cdc.gov/

American Heart Association (AHA). (2023). Plant-Based Diets. Retrieved from https://www.heart.org/

Crocker, J. (2019). Vegan Slow Cooking for Two or Just for You. Fair Winds Press.

Robertson, R. (2015). Fresh from the Vegan Slow Cooker: 200 Ultra-Convenient, Super-Tasty, Completely Animal-Free One-Dish Dinners. Harvard Common Press.

Appendix 1: Measurement Conversion Chart

U.S. System	Metric
1 inch	2.54 centimeters
1 fluid ounce	29.57 milliliters
1 pint (16 ounces)	473.18 milliliters, 2 cups
1 quart (32 ounces)	1 liter, 4 cups
1 gallon (128 ounces)	4 liters, 16 cups
1 pound (16 ounces)	437.5 grams (0.4536 kilogram), 473.18 milliliters
1 ounces	2 tablespoons, 28 grams
1 cup (8 ounces)	237 milliliters
1 teaspoon	5 milliliters
1 tablespoon	15 milliliters (3 teaspoons)
Fahrenheit (subtract 32 and divide by 1.8 to get Celsius)	Centigrade (multiply by 1.8 and add 32 to get Fahrenheit)

Appendix 2: Index Recipes

A

Acorn Squash
Stuffed Squash with Wild Rice - 37
Maple Glazed Acorn Squash - 49

Almond
Almond Banana Millet Mash - 12
Strawberry Basil Chia Pudding - 16
Slow-Roasted Spiced Nuts - 20
Savory Green Bean Almondine - 46
Spiced Basmati Rice Medley - 47

Almond Butter
Almond Butter Fudge Brownies - 79
Almond Banana Millet Mash - 12
Almond Butter Fudge Brownies - 79

Almond Milk
Almond Banana Millet Mash - 12
Peanut Butter Cacao Oats - 14
Warm Fig & Hazelnut Farro - 15
Strawberry Basil Chia Pudding - 16
Apple Pie Cauliflower Bowl - 17
Lavender Vanilla Barley Bowl - 18
Cashew Carrot Spread - 25
Sweet Potato Corn Chowder - 29
Zucchini Basil Bisque - 33
Roasted Red Pepper Soup - 34
Lentil & Root Veg Shepherd's Pie - 37
Tofu and Veggie Stroganoff - 38
Slow-Cooked Eggplant Parmesan - 39
Cheesy Vegan Cauliflower Gratin - 43
Creamy Tomato Penne Bake - 68
Choco-Chia Pudding Cake - 77
Slow-Cooked Choco Banana Bread - 79
Orange Cranberry Bread Pudding - 80
Carrot Cake Oat Bars - 81
Vegan Chocolate Lava Pots - 81

Amaranth
Spiced Pumpkin Amaranth Porridge - 12

Apple
Butternut Squash Apple Soup - 31
Cinnamon Apple Buckwheat Bowl - 11
Spiced Apple Cobbler - 78

Apple Cider Vinegar
Apple Cider Brussels Sprouts - 47

Artichoke
Vegan Spinach Artichoke Dip - 25

Avocado
Cabbage & Avocado Wrap - 76
Vegan Chickpea Bake with Avocado - 75

B

Banana
Almond Banana Millet Mash - 12
Banana Bread Breakfast Oats - 16
Slow-Cooked Choco Banana Bread - 79

Barley
Barley and Vegetable Pilaf - 61
Lavender Vanilla Barley Bowl - 18
Portobello and Barley Bake - 42

Basil
Strawberry Basil Chia Pudding - 16
Zucchini Basil Bisque - 33
Pesto Pasta with White Beans - 68

Basmati Rice
Spiced Basmati Rice Medley - 47

Bell Pepper
Italian Vegan Stuffed Peppers - 72
Roasted Red Pepper Hummus - 26
Stuffed Bell Pepper Scoops - 21
Zesty Lentil Poppers - 24
Jalapeño Corn Dip - 24
Thai-Inspired Coconut Soup - 29
Spicy Brown Rice & Mushroom Stew - 30
Italian White Bean Stew - 32
Roasted Red Pepper Soup - 34
Vegan Jambalaya - 42
Thai Red Lentil Curry - 52
Spicy Black Bean Chili - 52
Jamaican Jerk Veggie Stew - 53
Smoky Tempeh Chili - 56
Green Thai Vegetable Curry - 56
Cajun Black-Eyed Peas - 57
Cuban Mojo Black Beans - 58
Cajun Red Beans and Rice - 61
Mexican-Spiced Lentil Medley - 62
Spaghetti Squash Primavera - 64
Thai Peanut Noodle Bowl - 65
Teriyaki Udon Stir-Fry - 67
Zesty Lentil Taco Filling - 72
Cashew Cream Enchiladas - 73

Black Beans
Stuffed Bell Pepper Scoops - 21
Cuban Mojo Black Beans - 58
Spicy Black Bean Chili - 52
Slow-Cooked Salsa Dip - 22
Cashew Cream Enchiladas - 73
Black-Eyed Peas
Cajun Black-Eyed Peas - 57
Black Garlic
Black Garlic Veggie Broth - 35
Blueberry
Blueberry Lemon Breakfast Quinoa - 13
Warm Blueberry Crumble - 82
Bok Choy
Ginger Sesame Bok Choy - 48
Broccoli
Creamy Broccoli & Pea Soup - 30
Green Thai Vegetable Curry - 56
Tempeh and Broccoli Stir Bowl - 70
Teriyaki Udon Stir-Fry - 67
Brown Rice
Stuffed Bell Pepper Scoops - 21
Vegan Jambalaya - 42
Spicy Brown Rice & Mushroom Stew - 30
Brown Rice & Pinto Bowl - 59
Cajun Red Beans and Rice - 61
Brussels Sprouts
Apple Cider Brussels Sprouts - 47
Buckwheat
Cinnamon Apple Buckwheat Bowl - 11
Butternut Squash
Butternut Chickpea Curry - 54
Butternut Squash Apple Soup - 31
Butternut Squash Shells - 66
Jamaican Jerk Veggie Stew - 53
Vegan Moroccan Tagine - 71

C

Cabbage
Cabbage & Avocado Wrap - 76
Cabbage and Fennel Soup - 35
Slow Cooker Stuffed Cabbage Rolls - 43
Cajun Seasoning
Cajun Black-Eyed Peas - 57
Cajun Red Beans and Rice - 61
Cannellini Beans
Herb & Olive Bean Medley - 22
Smoky Cannellini with Spinach - 60
Carrot
Zesty Lentil Poppers - 24
Carrot Cake Oat Bars - 81
Cashew Carrot Spread - 25
Rustic Tomato Lentil Soup - 28
Italian White Bean Stew - 32
Curried Carrot Ginger Soup - 33
Kale & Potato Comfort Stew - 34
Cabbage and Fennel Soup - 35
Black Garlic Veggie Broth - 35
Rustic Tofu Pot Roast - 36
Lentil & Root Veg Shepherd's Pie - 37
Tofu and Veggie Stroganoff - 38
Slow Cooker Stuffed Cabbage Rolls - 43
Sweet & Spicy Glazed Carrots - 45
Smoky Cannellini with Spinach - 60
Barley and Vegetable Pilaf - 61
Thai Peanut Noodle Bowl - 65
Teriyaki Udon Stir-Fry - 67
Braised Tofu with Root Veggies - 69
Vegan Moroccan Tagine - 71
Spiced Tofu Veggie Loaf - 74
Cashew
Slow-Roasted Spiced Nuts - 20
Vegan Spinach Artichoke Dip - 25
Cashew Carrot Spread - 25
Pesto Pasta with White Beans - 68
Cashew Cream Enchiladas - 73
Creamy Cashew Cauliflower Curry - 55
Cauliflower
Apple Pie Cauliflower Bowl - 17
Balsamic Glazed Cauliflower Steaks - 41
Buffalo Cauliflower Bites - 20
Cheesy Vegan Cauliflower Gratin - 43
Creamy Cashew Cauliflower Curry - 55
Garlic Roasted Cauliflower Rice - 45
Celery
Black Garlic Veggie Broth - 35
Vegan Jambalaya - 42
Cajun Black-Eyed Peas - 57
Cajun Red Beans and Rice - 61
Spiced Tofu Veggie Loaf - 74
Cherry Tomatoes
Mediterranean Chickpea Bake - 38
Pesto Pasta with White Beans - 68
Italian Vegan Stuffed Peppers - 72
Vegan Stuffed Eggplant Boats - 73

Chia
Choco-Chia Pudding Cake - 77
Maple Chia Oatmeal Delight - 11
Spiced Pumpkin Amaranth Porridge - 12
Strawberry Basil Chia Pudding - 16
Chickpea
Butternut Chickpea Curry - 54
Chickpea Tikka Masala - 51
Mediterranean Chickpea Bake - 38
Moroccan Chickpea Stew - 31
Roasted Red Pepper Hummus - 26
Smoky Maple Chickpeas - 19
Herb & Olive Bean Medley - 22
Savory Chickpeas with Wild Rice - 60
Vegan Stuffed Eggplant Boats - 73
Vegan Chickpea Bake with Avocado - 75
Vegan Moroccan Tagine - 71
Cabbage & Avocado Wrap - 76
Chocolate
Choco-Chia Pudding Cake - 77
Vegan Chocolate Lava Pots - 81
Cinnamon
Cinnamon Apple Buckwheat Bowl - 11
Cinnamon Pear Compote - 82
Spiced Apple Cobbler - 78
Coconut Vanilla Rice Pudding - 80
Cocoa Powder
Peanut Butter Cacao Oats - 14
Choco-Chia Pudding Cake - 77
Slow-Cooked Choco Banana Bread - 79
Almond Butter Fudge Brownies - 79
Vegan Chocolate Lava Pots - 81
Coconut
Coconut Curry Popcorn Mix - 26
Coconut Date Breakfast Rice - 14
Coconut Vanilla Rice Pudding - 80
Coconut Milk
Creamy Coconut Quinoa Porridge - 10
Coconut Date Breakfast Rice - 14
Tropical Mango Quinoa Mash - 17
Thai-Inspired Coconut Soup - 29
Chickpea Tikka Masala - 51
Thai Red Lentil Curry - 52
Coconut Sweet Potato Curry - 53
Maple Pecan Sticky Rice - 78
Coconut Vanilla Rice Pudding - 80
Orange Cranberry Bread Pudding - 80

Corn
Stuffed Bell Pepper Scoops - 21
Slow-Cooked Salsa Dip - 22
Jalapeño Corn Dip - 24
Sweet Potato Corn Chowder - 29
Cranberry
Orange Cranberry Bread Pudding - 80

D
Date
Coconut Date Breakfast Rice - 14
Dill
Lemon Dill Split Pea Soup - 32

E
Edamame
Ginger-Garlic Edamame - 21
Eggplant
Slow-Cooked Eggplant Parmesan - 39
Creamy Polenta with Ratatouille - 40
Vegan Stuffed Eggplant Boats - 73

F
Farro
Lemony Farro and Fava Beans - 59
Warm Fig & Hazelnut Farro - 15
Fava Beans
Lemony Farro and Fava Beans - 59
Fennel
Cabbage and Fennel Soup - 35
Fig
Warm Fig & Hazelnut Farro - 15
Fingerling Potato
Rosemary Garlic Fingerlings - 50
Fusilli Pasta
Pesto Pasta with White Beans - 68

G
Garlic
Garlic Alfredo Zucchini Pasta - 64
Garlic Roasted Cauliflower Rice - 45
Ginger-Garlic Edamame - 21
Roasted Red Pepper Hummus - 26
BBQ Pulled Mushroom Sliders - 27
Caramelized Onion Bruschetta - 27
Rustic Tomato Lentil Soup - 28

Sweet Potato Corn Chowder - 29
Thai-Inspired Coconut Soup - 29
Spicy Brown Rice & Mushroom Stew - 30
Creamy Broccoli & Pea Soup - 30
Italian White Bean Stew - 32
Zucchini Basil Bisque - 33
Curried Carrot Ginger Soup - 33
Roasted Red Pepper Soup - 34
Kale & Potato Comfort Stew - 34
Rustic Tofu Pot Roast - 36
Tofu and Veggie Stroganoff - 38
Rosemary Garlic Fingerlings - 50
Lemon Garlic Orzo - 67
Lemon Garlic Tempeh Strips - 76

Ginger(fresh)
Curried Carrot Ginger Soup - 33
Ginger Sesame Bok Choy - 48
Ginger Turmeric Lentils - 58
Ginger-Garlic Edamame - 21

Green Beans
Savory Green Bean Almondine - 46

H

Hazelnut
Warm Fig & Hazelnut Farro - 15

J

Jalapeño
Jalapeño Corn Dip - 24

Jasmine Rice
Coconut Date Breakfast Rice - 14

K

Kale
Kale & Potato Comfort Stew - 34
Caramelized Onion and Kale - 49
White Bean & Kale Chili - 54

Kidney Beans
Herb & Olive Bean Medley - 22
Jamaican Jerk Veggie Stew - 53
Cajun Red Beans and Rice - 3

L

Lasagna Noodles
Slow-Cooked Lasagna Roll-Ups - 65

Lavender
Lavender Vanilla Barley Bowl - 18

Lemon
Blueberry Lemon Breakfast Quinoa - 13
Lemon Dill Split Pea Soup - 32
Lemon Garlic Orzo - 67
Lemon Herb Quinoa Pilaf - 44
Lemony Farro and Fava Beans - 59

Lentil
Ethiopian Berbere Lentils - 55
Ginger Turmeric Lentils - 58
Lentil & Root Veg Shepherd's Pie - 37
Mexican-Spiced Lentil Medley - 62
Rustic Tomato Lentil Soup - 28
Spaghetti Squash with Lentil Sauce - 70
Thai Red Lentil Curry - 52
Zesty Lentil Poppers - 24
Zesty Lentil Taco Filling - 72
Slow Cooker Stuffed Cabbage Rolls - 43
Italian Vegan Stuffed Peppers - 72
Slow Cooker Vegan "Meatballs" - 75

M

Mango
Tropical Mango Quinoa Mash - 17

Maple Syrup
Maple BBQ Seitan Medallions - 71
Maple Chia Oatmeal Delight - 11
Maple Glazed Acorn Squash - 49
Maple Pecan Sticky Rice - 78
Smoky Maple Chickpeas - 19
Sweet Potato Pie Oats - 18
Slow-Roasted Spiced Nuts - 20
Sticky Sesame Mushrooms - 23
Coconut Curry Popcorn Mix - 26
Caramelized Onion Bruschetta - 27
Sweet & Spicy Glazed Carrots - 45
Apple Cider Brussels Sprouts - 47
Miso Glazed Sweet Potatoes - 74
Slow-Cooked Choco Banana Bread - 79
Spiced Apple Cobbler - 78
Almond Butter Fudge Brownies - 79
Coconut Vanilla Rice Pudding - 80
Carrot Cake Oat Bars - 81
Warm Blueberry Crumble - 82

Millet
Almond Banana Millet Mash - 12
Vanilla Pear Millet Bowl - 15

Miso Paste
Miso Glazed Sweet Potatoes - 74
Mushroom
BBQ Pulled Mushroom Sliders - 27
Mushroom Bourguignon - 39
Spicy Brown Rice & Mushroom Stew - 30
Sticky Sesame Mushrooms - 23
Wild Mushroom Rice Blend - 50
Thai-Inspired Coconut Soup - 29
Portobello and Barley Bake - 42
Mushroom Stroganoff Pasta - 66
Slow Cooker Vegan "Meatballs" - 75

O

Onion
BBQ Pulled Mushroom Sliders - 27
Caramelized Onion and Kale - 49
Caramelized Onion Bruschetta - 27
Rustic Tomato Lentil Soup - 28
Sweet Potato Corn Chowder - 29
Thai-Inspired Coconut Soup - 29
Italian White Bean Stew - 32
Curried Carrot Ginger Soup - 33
Roasted Red Pepper Soup - 34
Kale & Potato Comfort Stew - 34
Black Garlic Veggie Broth - 35
Rustic Tofu Pot Roast - 36
Lentil & Root Veg Shepherd's Pie - 37
Tofu and Veggie Stroganoff - 38
Mediterranean Chickpea Bake - 38
Vegan Jambalaya - 42
Thai Red Lentil Curry - 52
Cajun Black-Eyed Peas - 57
Cuban Mojo Black Beans - 58
Zesty Lentil Taco Filling - 72
Slow Cooker Vegan "Meatballs" - 75
Orange
Orange Cranberry Bread Pudding - 80
Orzo
Lemon Garlic Orzo - 67

P

Parsnips
Braised Tofu with Root Veggies - 69
Creamy Mashed Parsnips - 46
Pasta Shells
Butternut Squash Shells - 66

Pea
Creamy Broccoli & Pea Soup - 30
Lemon Dill Split Pea Soup - 32
Creamy Vegan Mac & Peas - 63
Peanut
Sweet Potato and Peanut Casserole - 40
Peanut Butter
Peanut Butter Cacao Oats - 14
Sweet Potato and Peanut Casserole - 40
Thai Peanut Noodle Bowl - 65
Pear
Cinnamon Pear Compote - 82
Vanilla Pear Millet Bowl - 15
Pecan
Maple Pecan Sticky Rice - 78
Warm Blueberry Crumble - 82
Penne pasta
Creamy Tomato Penne Bake - 68
Pinto Beans
Brown Rice & Pinto Bowl - 59
Polenta
Creamy Polenta with Ratatouille - 40
Popcorn
Coconut Curry Popcorn Mix - 26
Potato
Kale & Potato Comfort Stew - 34
Rustic Tofu Pot Roast - 36
Pumpkin Purée
Spiced Pumpkin Amaranth Porridge - 12

Q

Quinoa
Blueberry Lemon Breakfast Quinoa - 13
Creamy Coconut Quinoa Porridge - 3
Tropical Mango Quinoa Mash - 10
Sweet Potato Tot Cups - 23
Slow Cooker Stuffed Cabbage Rolls - 43
Lemon Herb Quinoa Pilaf - 44
Sun-Dried Tomato Quinoa - 62
Italian Vegan Stuffed Peppers - 72
Vegan Stuffed Eggplant Boats - 73

R

Rolled Oats
Banana Bread Breakfast Oats - 16
Carrot Cake Oat Bars - 81
Golden Turmeric Oats - 13

Maple Chia Oatmeal Delight - 11
Peanut Butter Cacao Oats - 14
Sweet Potato Pie Oats - 18
Apple Pie Cauliflower Bowl - 17
Zesty Lentil Poppers - 24
Spiced Tofu Veggie Loaf - 74
Slow Cooker Vegan "Meatballs" - 75
Warm Blueberry Crumble - 82
Rosemary (fresh)
Rosemary Garlic Fingerlings - 50
Rotini Pasta
Mushroom Stroganoff Pasta - 66

S

Seitan
Maple BBQ Seitan Medallions - 71
Sesame oil
Sticky Sesame Mushrooms - 23
Ginger Sesame Bok Choy - 48
Sesame seeds
Sticky Sesame Mushrooms - 23
Ginger Sesame Bok Choy - 48
Spaghetti
Thai Peanut Noodle Bowl - 65
Spaghetti Squash
Spaghetti Squash Primavera - 64
Spaghetti Squash with Lentil Sauce - 70
Spinach
Vegan Spinach Artichoke Dip - 25
Smoky Cannellini with Spinach - 60
Slow-Cooked Lasagna Roll-Ups - 65
Cashew Cream Enchiladas - 73
Strawberry
Strawberry Basil Chia Pudding - 16
Sun-Dried Tomato
Sun-Dried Tomato Quinoa - 62
Sweet Potato
Miso Glazed Sweet Potatoes - 74
Sweet Potato Corn Chowder - 29
Sweet Potato Pie Oats - 18
Sweet Potato Tot Cups - 23
Lentil & Root Veg Shepherd's Pie - 37
Sweet Potato and Peanut Casserole - 40
Herbed Sweet Potato Mash - 48
Coconut Sweet Potato Curry - 53
Braised Tofu with Root Veggies - 69

T

Tamari
Tamari Tempeh & Veggie Skillet - 41
Tempeh
Lemon Garlic Tempeh Strips - 76
Smoky Tempeh Chili - 56
Tamari Tempeh & Veggie Skillet - 41
Tempeh and Broccoli Stir Bowl - 70
Teriyaki
Teriyaki Udon Stir-Fry - 67
Tofu
Braised Tofu with Root Veggies - 69
Rustic Tofu Pot Roast - 36
Slow Cooker Vegan "Meatballs" - 75
Slow-Cooked Lasagna Roll-Ups - 65
Spiced Tofu Veggie Loaf - 74
Tofu and Veggie Stroganoff - 38
Tomato
Creamy Tomato Penne Bake - 68
Rustic Tomato Lentil Soup - 28
Turmeric
Ginger Turmeric Lentils - 58
Golden Turmeric Oats - 13

U

Udon Noodles
Teriyaki Udon Stir-Fry - 67

V

Vanilla Extract
Coconut Vanilla Rice Pudding - 80
Lavender Vanilla Barley Bowl - 18
Vanilla Pear Millet Bowl - 15
Maple Pecan Sticky Rice - 78
Almond Butter Fudge Brownies - 79

W

Walnuts
Slow-Roasted Spiced Nuts - 20
Spiced Apple Cobbler - 78
Carrot Cake Oat Bars - 81
White Bean
Italian White Bean Stew - 32
Pesto Pasta with White Beans - 68
White Bean & Kale Chili - 54

White Rice
Wild Mushroom Rice Blend - **50**
Maple Pecan Sticky Rice - **78**
Coconut Vanilla Rice Pudding - **80**
Wild Rice
Savory Chickpeas with Wild Rice - **60**
Stuffed Squash with Wild Rice - **37**
Wild Mushroom Rice Blend - **50**

Z

Zucchini
Garlic Alfredo Zucchini Pasta - **64**
Zucchini Basil Bisque - **33**
Rustic Tomato Lentil Soup - **28**
Spicy Brown Rice & Mushroom Stew - **30**
Italian White Bean Stew - **32**
Mediterranean Chickpea Bake - **38**
Creamy Polenta with Ratatouille - **40**
Green Thai Vegetable Curry - **56**
Lemony Farro and Fava Beans - **59**
Barley and Vegetable Pilaf - **61**
Mexican-Spiced Lentil Medley - **62**
Spaghetti Squash Primavera - **64**
Slow-Cooked Lasagna Roll-Ups - **65**
Creamy Tomato Penne Bake - **68**
Italian Vegan Stuffed Peppers - **721**

Notes

TABLE OF CONTENT ◊ 97

Printed in Dunstable, United Kingdom